The Mahabharata

THE CHARACTERS

VYASA	The whole story is told by an author-narrator, VYASA, who frequently takes part in his own story.
GANESHA	VYASA is assisted by a divine scribe, GANESHA, who has an elephant's head on a human body. GANESHA writes down everything VYASA says.
SANTANU	At the beginning of the family of the BHARATAS, a king called SANTANU takes, as his first wife, GANGA, who gives him a wonderful son, BHISMA, the most perfect man.
BHISMA	BHISMA, to allow his father to marry a second time, solemnly swears to renounce the love of a woman. As a reward for this vow, he receives from the gods the power to choose the day of his death. A revered and immortal warrior, he is present throughout the story. In the last part, he is almost a hundred years old.
SATYAVATI	For his second wife, SANTANU takes SATYAVATI, who was born in a fish. At the time of her marriage to SANTANU, SATYAVATI is already the mother of VYASA, the author of the poem, who has very close family ties with his own characters. SANTANU and SATYAVATI have a sickly son who dies childless, leaving two young widows. So that the poem may continue, VYASA gives children to the two young princesses. From these unions are born two sons, DHRITARASHTRA and PANDU.
DHRITHARASHTRA	DHRITHARASHTRA, the first born, is blind. He marries a princess called GANDHARI, and from this union come a hundred sons, the KAURAVAS.
DURYODHANA	DURYODHANA is the first born of these hundred sons. He passionately desires the rulership of the earth.
DUSHASSANA	DURYODHANA is supported by his brothers (among whom the vicious DUSHASSANA is noticeable) and by a fearsome warrior, of seemingly humble origin, KARNA.
KARNA	KARNA is in reality the son of a princess called KUNTI and the sun. She had this son at the age of fifteen.
KUNTI PANDU	It is KUNTI who marries the second brother, PANDU. He takes a second wife, called MADRI. But PANDU is stricken by

MADRI	a curse and the intervention of the gods is necessary in order that the two women may bear sons. KUNTI gives birth to three sons and MADRI to twin sons. These five brothers, the sons of PANDU, call themselves the PANDAVAS.
YUDHISHTHIRA	The first of the five brothers is called YUDHISHTHIRA. He is the son of KUNTI and of DHARMA, the god of earthly harmony.
BHIMA	The second is BHIMA, son of KUNTI and of VAYU, the god of the wind. He is the strongest man in the world.
ARJUNA	The third brother, ARJUNA, son of KUNTI and of the king of the gods, INDRA, is the finest archer and the greatest conqueror in the world.
NAKULA and SAHADEVA	The other two brothers, who symbolise patience and wisdom, are NAKULA and SAHADEVA. They are the sons of MADRI and of the ASHWINS, the twin gods.
DRAUPADI	These five brothers marry one and the same woman, DRAUPADI. She gives them each a son. The five PANDAVAS and the hundred KAURAVAS are therefore first cousins, the off-spring of two brothers. They are brought up together under the guidance of the elderly BHISMA. As for KARNA, ARJUNA's direct rival, he is – for his mother is KUNTI – the elder brother of the PANDAVAS. But, until a certain point in the story, he is unaware of his origin.
DRONA	Two other characters play an important role in the destiny of the BHARATAS. The first is called DRONA. He is a very knowledgeable Brahmin who has subsequently become the greatest master of arms. He has a son called ASHWATTHAMAN.
KRISHNA	The second is KRISHNA himself, friend of the PANDAVAS and particularly of ARJUNA. ARJUNA takes KRISHNA's sister, SUBHADRA, as his second wife. KRISHNA isn't officially a king but his prestige is considerable. He is the earthly incarnation (an avatar) of the great god VISHNU. It is necessary to mention also SHAKUNI the trickster, brother of GANDHARI; AMBA, a princess rejected by BHISMA whom she pursues through all the world, and two young characters with tragic fates: ABHIMANYU, son of ARJUNA and SUBHADRA, and GHATOTKACHA, son of BHIMA and a demoness.

THE MAHABHARATA

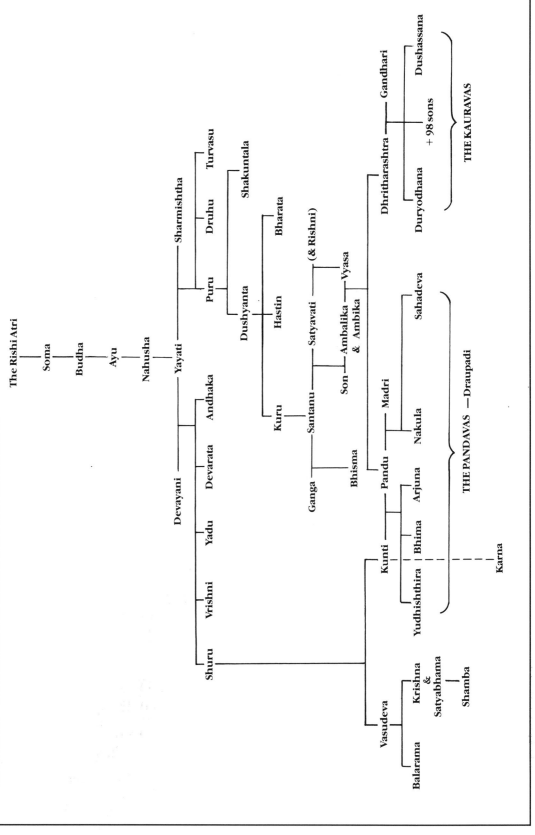

The game of dice

A poet-narrator called Vyasa announces to a child that he is going to tell him the history of his race and that this story is 'the poetical history of mankind'.

Enter Ganesha, the god with an elephant's head, who offers himself as writer of this great poem. Questioned by the child, he explains how he came to have the head of an elephant. Then he settles down to write.

Vyasa begins with the story of his own birth. He then plays the part of his first protagonist, King Santanu and relates the birth of a wonderful son, called Bhisma.

Twenty years later, Santanu falls in love with another woman, Satyavati, the poet Vyasa's own mother. Her father, in agreeing to her marriage with Santanu, demands that their son be the future king. Santanu cannot accept, for he already has a son, Bhisma. Whereupon Bhisma, for love of his father, vows that, so as never to have a child, he will remain celibate.

Santanu then marries Satyavati. They have a son who is of such poor health that he is unable to win a wife at a tournament, as was the custom. So Bhisma fights on behalf of his half-brother and returns with three brides instead of one. One of them, Amba, is already secretly engaged. Bhisma lets her go but her betrothed does not want her any more. Alone and forlorn she returns to Bhisma and demands that he marry her.

Bhisma, faithful to his vow, refuses. Amba then swears that one day she will kill him. The gods, however, have given Bhisma the power to choose the day of his death, therefore he cannot be killed. Nevertheless, Amba swears that she will find a way to kill him.

The young king dies childless. Is the poetical history of mankind over so soon, for want of protagonists? The young princesses must be given children. But who can father them? The only man in the family is Bhisma, and he has renounced women.

Satyavati then asks her first son, Vyasa himself, to give children to the two princesses. The author of the poem performs his duty but the princesses flinch from contact with him, for he is filthy and smells. He then explains to them that they will each bear a son, but that the first will be born blind because the first princess closed her eyes on seeing him, and that the second will be pale-skinned, because the second princess blanched at his touch.

These two sons are called Dhritharashtra – the blind, and Pandu – the pale. Pandu is king, but he is at once cursed by a gazelle which he killed while it was enjoying the pleasures of love: if he makes love to either of his two wives (Kunti and Madri) he will immediately die.

He goes away with his wives to the mountains. Kunti, his first wife, informs him that she possesses a magic power. She can invoke a god at will and have a child by him. Straight away, this power is put to the test and three sons are born to her: Yudhishthira, the first born, truthful and scrupulous, son of Dharma, Bhima, the strongest of men, and Arjuna, the conqueror.

Madri, Pandu's second wife, makes use of this power too. She gives birth to twin sons, Nakula and Sahadeva. Thanks to his two wives, Pandu has five sons descended from the gods – the Pandavas.

Following his brother's exile, Dhritharashtra has become king, despite his blindness. He marries Gandhari, who, on learning of her husband's infirmity, decides to cover her eyes with a bandage which she will never remove. Then, after an unnaturally long pregnancy she becomes, by extraordinary means, the mother of a hundred sons, the Kauravas. The first born is called Duryodhana. He brings with him hate and destruction.

Pandu dies because, one spring day, he prefers love to life. The first age of the world is coming to an end. A terrible, world-wide, incomprehensible war approaches.

Bhisma, by now an old man, decides to bring up the two sets of cousins, the Pandavas and the Kauravas, together. But everything tears them apart. Ever since their youth they have been trying to kill each other.

Enter Drona, a prodigious master of arms, who discovers in Arjuna an extremely gifted archer. He promises to make him the best, not shrinking from asking a young rival, who calls himself his pupil, to cut off his thumb so that he will lose his skill and his strength.

During the course of an archery tournament, Arjuna's superiority is suddenly tested by a very dangerous newcomer called Karna. Welcomed by Duryodhana and consecrated king by him, Karna swears eternal friendship.

Karna is in reality – as we learn from Vyasa – Kunti's first-born child, the result of her union with the sun. He is therefore the unknown brother of the Pandavas, against whom he will one day fight to the death.

The five Pandavas marry. As a result of their mother's unguarded words, they take for their wife Draupadi, who binds them together irrevocably. And, as the bad omens gather, Krishna makes his appearance. It is said he is the incarnation of the god Vishnu, come down to save the earth from chaos.

On his advice, the Pandavas go before the blind king. Yudhishthira, in spite of the exclamations of his brother Bhima, accepts a worthless part of the kingdom, in the hope of averting a war which all feel to be unavoidable.

Several years pass happily. Yudhishthira can well imagine that Vyasa's great poem is finished. But this is only the beginning. He must now be crowned king of kings.

Duryodhana, the eldest of the Kauravas, cannot stand the wisdom and power of Yudhishthira. He follows the advice of his uncle, the cunning Shakuni, feared player of dice, and invites Yudhishthira to a game, knowing that gambling is his weakness. Yudhishthira accepts. Carried away by the intoxication of the game (or for other, secret reasons) he loses his entire possessions, his lands, his kingdom, even his brothers, even himself, even Draupadi, their joint wife, who is dragged before the company. She is about to be stripped naked, when she invokes Krishna, who comes to her rescue. She swears that one day death will avenge her. There will be a war, merciless war.

It is perhaps in order to avert this war that Yudhishthira agrees to a last match, a kind of double or quits. Once again, he loses. The Pandavas and Draupadi are condemned to spend twelve years in exile in the forest, and a thirteenth year in an unknown place, disguised so that no one may recognise them.

They leave. Vyasa describes their departure to the blind king and queen.

Exile in the forest

While the Kauravas are uneasy in their palace, the Pandavas have withdrawn into the forest. There, they encounter Amba, she who once swore to kill Bhisma, and is desperately trying to find someone to perform the impossible task.

A mysterious voice in the forest tells her that nothing can outwit death 'except death itself'. She leaves.

Draupadi and Bhima then reproach Yudhishthira for his inaction, his passivity. Wouldn't it be better, since it is obvious Shakuni cheated at dice, to rise up and fight? Yudhishthira flatly refuses. He will keep his word. He will follow his *dharma*.

Arjuna then leaves. He is aiming for the high mountains to look for the divine weapons which one day they will need.

He leaves Draupadi under the protection of his brothers.

Night falls. Bhima keeps watch while the others sleep. Enter a Rakshasha, a creature of the night. She falls madly in love with Bhima who fights with her brother and kills him. Then he sires a child on the magical creature. This child, who is called Ghatotkatcha, swears he will one day rise up and come to the aid of his father.

The Kauravas have come right into the forest. Dushassana, Duryodhana's vicious brother, wants to destroy the Pandavas, but they are saved by Vyasa himself.

In the palace, Kunti and Gandhari, the two mothers, are worried. Kunti tries to convince her unacknowledged son, Karna, not to take part in the war. But she fails.

Duryodhana wants to know the reason for Arjuna's expedition. He evokes him by magic. They see Arjuna fighting with a mysterious hunter, who turns out to be the god Shiva himself. Shiva gives Arjuna Pasupata, the supreme weapon, which may destroy the world.

Moreover, in the heavens, a seductive creature approaches Arjuna and offers herself to him. He refuses and she curses him: one day he will lose his virility and he will be like a woman. His enemies, who have witnessed this scene by magic, ask themselves whether it isn't at that moment that they should attack and destroy him.

One day, the Pandavas, still in exile, are killed by the waters of a poisonous lake. Yudhishthira, however, brings his brothers back to life by correctly answering the questions which the lake puts to him. Now they must find a place to hide for one year. Dharma tells them to choose the disguise of their most secret desire.

Meanwhile, Karna, having promised Duryodhana victory, decides he too must acquire the absolute weapon. Danger grows

ever closer, ever more menacing. For many months Karna has served an all-powerful hermit, the destroyer of warriors. As a reward, he bestows upon Karna, whom he takes to be a servant, the absolute weapon. But Karna, by an excess of fortitude (he does not cry when a worm bores a hole in his thigh) shows himself to be a warrior. The hermit curses him and predicts that the moment he wishes for the weapon he will forget the secret formula and that will be the moment of his death.

According to the conditions of the dice-game, the year which the Pandavas are to spend in disguise has now arrived. Yudhishthira, who appears as a poor Brahmin, and his brothers and Draupadi, who pass for wandering servants, find asylum at the court of King Virata. There, they tell how Bhima, during the course of his stay in the forest, encountered his half-brother Hanuman, the miraculous monkey, whose tail he was not able to lift. On this occasion, Yudhishthira announces the coming of a dark age, the age of Kali (Kali-yuga).

At the court of this king, a general, called Kitchaka, becomes infatuated with Draupadi, and does everything he can to possess her, even threatening her life. Draupadi implores mighty Bhima to help her and so he goes in her stead to a love-tryst and pulverises the too-amorous general.

Meanwhile, Duryodhana has launched an attack upon Virata's kingdom. The king places his troops in the hands of his young son, Uttara, who, however, declares he has no driver for his chariot. Draupadi – who seeks war at all cost – points out Arjuna as the best driver in the world, although he has taken the appearance of a transvestite and dance instructor. The Pandavas reveal their true identity somewhat before the agreed time.

War is nigh. Duryodhana does not want to give his cousins their kingdom because they came out of hiding before the appointed time. He goes to request Krishna's support. Arjuna does the same. Arjuna chooses Krishna himself, alone and unarmed, and lets Duryodhana have all of Krishna's armies. He asks him to drive his chariot. Krishna accepts.

In the Kauravas' palace, the blind king, who is intimidated by his sons, also senses the coming of war. He asks the elderly Bhisma, the incomparable warrior, to take the supreme command. Bhisma accepts, against his will, but on one condition: that Karna does not fight. Although very displeased, Karna agrees only to fight after Bhisma's death.

Krishna comes forth as a peacemaker. He speaks to Duryodhana, who does not listen to him. He reveals his universal form, which is only visible to those who have eyes to see. He speaks to Bhisma, who is bound to the Kauravas. He speaks to Kunti, who does everything to push her sons into war. Finally, he speaks to Karna, going so far as to reveal to him that he is the brother of those whom he intends to fight. But Karna was abandoned by his mother at the very hour of his birth; he then has a vision of the end of the world. He will fight with the Kauravas, even though he can already foresee their defeat and his own death.

The war

*J*ust as the battle is about to start, Arjuna sees his relations against whom he is going to fight and breaks down. He refuses to fight. Krishna, who is his charioteer, addresses him as they stand in the no-man's-land between the two armies. This is the famous *Bhagavad Gita*, the guide to straightforward and resolute action.

Battle begins, but it is impossible to vanquish Bhisma. One evening in the camp, Bhisma receives a visit from the ghost of Amba. She comes to inform him of her death. She says that she threw herself into the fire and that she is now reborn as a man. His name is Sikhandin.

The Pandavas tell Bhisma that unless he is killed the war will go on until the end of the world. When asked how he can be vanquished, he replies: place Sikhandin in the front line and tell him to strike me.

The next day, facing Sikhandin, he makes one last challenge. But his will to live leaves him. He drops his weapons. An arrow hits him, shot not by Amba – Sikhandin, who has suddenly forgotten all the reasons for his hatred – but by Arjuna.

Bhisma does not die until later. He remains lying on a bed of arrows until the end of the battle. Now Karna enters the fray, and Duryodhana rejoices.

Drona, master of arms, takes command. He disposes the armies according to a formation known only to him, the iron disc, which no one knows how to break open. No one save Arjuna. If only Arjuna can be diverted from the battle, Drona guarantees victory.

Karna remains alone at night. Kunti goes up to him (she knows that he now intends to fight) wishing to persuade him to join the Pandavas. She confesses to being his mother and asks his forgiveness. But Karna is not to be moved. He will fight against his brothers. He does, however, promise Kunti that he will only kill Arjuna, for, as he says, one of them must die. Thus, after the battle she will have as many sons as before.

Arjuna has a second wife, Subhadra, Krishna's sister. They have a fifteen-year-old son, Abhimanyu, who, while still in his mother's womb heard his father speaking, thereby learning how to force a breach into Drona's battle-formation, the iron disk.

As Arjuna has been called to a battle far away, Yudhishthira entrusts Abhimanyu with the task of opening a breach in the disc. Abhimanyu succeeds brilliantly, but the break closes behind him and the others are unable to follow. Abhimanyu, despite his bravery, is slain.

Arjuna returns to the camp. Stricken with rage and grief by the sight of his dead son, he swears to avenge his dead son before sunset the next day.

The following day, Karna throws himself into the battle and fights brilliantly. A god once gave him a magic lance which will kill any living being but can only be used once. He is keeping this lance for Arjuna.

To dispose of this lance, Krishna calls on Ghatotkatcha, son of

Bhima and the creature of the night. He appears immediately to save his human family. At night, a terrible battle confronts Karna. He can only kill the demon by resorting to his magic lance which can only be used once. Ghatotkatcha is killed, but Krishna dances with joy. Karna is now vulnerable and Arjuna can kill him.

First it is necessary to kill Drona, an invincible warrior, surpassing even Arjuna himself. He can only be beaten through his weaknesses: his love for his son, Ashwatthaman, and a curse which is upon him. Bhima kills an elephant – also called Ashwatthaman – and deceitfully tells Drona of the death of his son. Drona, suspecting a lie, asks Yudhishthira for the truth. In order to save his armies, Yudhishthira is forced into a half-lie which distresses him. Drona feels his strength ebb and lets himself be killed.

Karna's hour has come. He sets out to fight weighed down by bad omens, and led by a disquieting charioteer who may be the god Shiva himself. He spares Yudhishthira, as he promised Kunti, and fends off Arjuna.

Meanwhile Bhima, grievously wounded, sees Dushassana coming towards him. He had once vowed to drink his blood and eat his guts and this he proceeds to do while Draupadi washes her hair in the dead man's blood.

Duryodhana asks Karna to avenge his brother Dushassana. Finally Karna confronts Arjuna in a crucial battle. It is the earth herself who, in seizing Karna's chariot-wheels, brings about his death. Karna tries to invoke the absolute weapon but the words escape him. He dies as the curse predicted.

It is now the turn of Duryodhana who refuses to surrender to the last. He hides at the bottom of a lake whose waters he has magically hardened. He only comes up to fight Bhima who kills him by treacherously striking him on the legs. As he lies dying, Ashwatthaman tells him how he penetrated into the camp of the conquering Pandavas in order to avenge Drona's death, and perpetrated a hideous and useless massacre leaving the Pandavas without descendants. Duryodhana dies content.

Bhisma, nearing his end, is brought back onto the battlefield. The Pandavas discover that Karna was Kunti's son and that he valued more highly his loyalty to Duryodhana than his family ties.

Yudhishthira thereupon decides to renounce the blood-stained throne and to withdraw to the woods. Draupadi urges him to stay. Bhisma speaks to him and shows him how, in the midst of the worst misfortunes, man always retains a slight hope and 'the taste for honey'. Then Bhisma dies, for his hour has come.

Gandhari curses Krishna whom she considers to be responsible for all that has befallen them. Calmly, Krishna accepts this curse. He tells Gandhari that one light has been saved even if she cannot see it. And Yudhishthira agrees to reign.

It is now Krishna's turn to die, very simply, killed by mistake in the forest. Before dying, he had time to save the child in the womb of Abhimanyu's young widow. From him is descended the child to whom the great story is told.

Thirty-six years have passed. The blind king, Gandhari and Kunti are on a river-bank. They speak of the past, of the unforgettable war. The king orders his wife to remove the bandage, just this once, before dying. She tells him she has taken it off but she keeps it on, faithful to her vow.

Then all three walk towards a fire which has broken out in the forest.

An aged Yudhishthira, carrying a dog in his arms, arrives in paradise. His brothers and Draupadi, who left the earth with him, have fallen into the abyss. A gatekeeper tells him to leave the dog behind if he wants to enter paradise. He refuses, but enters nonetheless, for this was a test.

In paradise, the 'inconceivable region', some surprises are still awaiting him. His enemies are there, smiling and happy. His brothers and Draupadi, on the other hand, seem to be in torment. Why? Yudhishthira asks himself these final questions before accepting peace at last, with the recognition that all is illusion.

The Mahabharata

PETER BROOK'S EPIC IN THE MAKING

Garry O'Connor
PHOTOGRAPHY BY GILLES ABEGG

HODDER & STOUGHTON
LONDON SYDNEY AUCKLAND TORONTO

British Library Cataloguing in Publication Data

O'Connor, Garry
    The Mahabharata.
    1. British cinema films. Mahabharata. Production
    I. Title
    791.43'72

    ISBN 0-340-50151-0

First published in Great Britain 1989

Published by Hodder & Stoughton,
a division of Hodder & Stoughton Ltd,
Mill Road, Dunton Green, Sevenoaks, Kent TN13 2YE
Editorial Office: 47 Bedford Square, London WC1B 3DP

Photoset by Litho Link Ltd, Welshpool, Powys, Wales.
Printed in Great Britain by Butler & Tanner, Frome and London.

To Victoria

A bird went by him like an arrow, something with a
story and a purpose, though it was a purpose of life.

G. K. Chesterton, *Life of St Francis*

CONTENTS

What is not here is nowhere . . .

Joinville Studios, 20 September 1988

*I*n the East of Paris, just the other side of the Forest of Vincennes, the studios of Joinville lie close to the Marne, with its river bank images of tranquil boating and picnicking, subjects of some of the most famous Impressionist paintings. A minute or two from a huge film processing plant and laboratory in the rue Charles Pathé, the man who gave his name to early black and white newsreels, the dilapidated stages of the studios stand back from the main shopping street. These more or less forgotten buildings have been home to some of the great masterpieces of the French cinema, but are now marked for demolition.

Plateau 32

Outside, the air is bracing, almost warm. A lanky, ebony-faced actor from Upper Volta sits spreadeagled in the sunshine, affectionately calling to the robed and skirted characters who sweep by.

I enter *Plateau 32*. The forbidding, heavily insulated door shuts silently behind me. I turn the corner of an avenue of tall, wood-strutted flats of canvas and suddenly I am in India, walking on uneven red dust and blinded by the glare, among strangely clad figures, men in terry-cotton robes or naked to the waist, in loose baggy leggings – their hair tied in pony-tails – women in blazing saffrons, or the revealing sackcloth of evil spirits. An elephant-headed scribe sits in a corner writing the story down.

India. But instead of the street vendors, hand-wheeled carts, honking taxis and raucous shouts of a Delhi market, this is an ancient India of mythical beginnings, a time when there was little distinction between men and gods. The fringes of this mythological world are inhabited with the more familiar gremlins of the cinema unit: assistants, cameramen, accountants, make-up artists, hairdressers, sound operators, with, in this case, Indian tailors flown specially from Bombay to hand-stitch the seams of the unusual costumes.

The actors are of all sizes, shapes, and colours, called upon to represent the almost impossible: heroes and heroines, men and women, still tied by a string to a male or female deity. Each adds a colour or stain to the great dome of *The Mahabharata*, the adaptation of the epic which lies at the very roots of India's mythology and religion, and which is now being assembled for filming in the Paris suburbs.

Someone massages the feet of the imperious, yet touchingly vulnerable and beautiful figure of the actress playing Draupadi, role model for all Indian women, ancient and modern alike. The gigantic grid in which they move, framed above by steel galleries like some mammoth set for life-size puppets, is of earthen ramparts, mounds and temples, columns and grottoes, palace courtyards and citadels. Each set will be demolished and become reborn in another form, until the last great battle when only the bare earth will remain . . .

A gentle but noble-faced prince greets me. Blond-haired, this is the Aryan king of kings, hero of the epic tale. His name is Yudhishthira. 'I try not to be more intelligent than these extraordinary characters,' he tells me in East-European tones. He is Polish, a famous romantic actor and film star in his own country.

Today they are filming 'The Game of Dice', the main turning-point of the story, the catastrophic event when Yudhishthira gambles away everything, including his brothers, and the wife all five hold in common – Draupadi.

Duryodhana, the evil antagonist to the hero, is engulfed by envy and has been driven mad to possess all he has: his divine, sublime

palace, his wealth, his wife –

I've seen all the kings of the earth surround Yudhishthira.
I've seen his people happy, even the aged, even the children . . .
I've seen a head sliced from a body with a flick of Krishna's
wrist . . .

But he knows the king of kings loves gambling, and challenged
to a game of dice he won't know how to refuse.

The setting for the game is, by the standards of this production,
elaborate. I approach the director. He is a small, tubby man, his head
almost bald, with ragged borders of white hair. He wears cheap,
comfortable shoes, a navy-blue donkey-jacket, and light-coloured
jeans. He has sharp, dancing blue eyes. Like ice-picks, someone once
said.

The director is preoccupied. He operates out of extreme
concentration, always speaking in a low voice and using simple
gestures. Dark and swarthy, the cameraman crouches on his dolly
like the Hunchback of Notre-Dame.

I ask the director about the lamps and carpet on which the dice-
table has been placed.

'You must speak to the designer,' he says. 'She is the real star of
this show.' He turns back to peer into a monitor beside the sound
technician.

Everyone has removed their shoes to tread over the carpet,
which is spread over a large platform of wooden rostrums all bolted
together. The whole preparation for this scene is an object lesson in
the management of illusion. The carpet has been hand-quilted so that
it has a special, individual light reflecting from it; the temple lamps
which hang around the gaming space are also hand-crafted – these are
called *diyas*. The walls of the great hall are pink.

The bulky cameraman confers with the lithe, fast-talking French-Canadian who masterminds the placing of the lights. The frame for the camera track is being dug into position in the sand by a multi-national, non-union team who work at ferocious speed with wedges and blocks of wood of every conceivable shape.

The *décorateur*, with a bucket, throws an extra coating of sand over the pillars; the *costumiers* carry over robes and gowns for the rival Kauravas and Pandavas, the clans of cousins whose conflict and its outcome will determine the fate of the world.

The third assistant director, an American, ear glued to his walkie-talkie, has twenty-two actors and actresses to get through costume and make-up – 'I don't have much time,' he tells me. Rushing is his whole being. So much for the oriental, meditative values of the East . . . This will always remain one of the paradoxes, or ironies, of this whole hypercharged, deeply occidental enterprise. The sultry continuity girl, puffing at a cigarette, does the day's tally of minutes of film shot, tape used, actor's attendance clocked up – everyone no doubt relishes the *heures supplémentaires*.

Two hours, and we are nearly ready for the first take of the day. I marvel at this daily setting up and pulling down: sometimes two or three times a day, although, for the most part, with less structurally dominating décors than the gaming-hall.

The director stands surveying the scene, reminding me, irreverently, of an Israeli corps commander on the battlefield. The dark-haired, gamine figure of his assistant stands by his side. Her taste in clothes is for cloaks, large earrings and pixie shoes. She is an unconventional aide-de-camp. The pair also makes me think of Prospero and Ariel . . .

The designer, a Greek lady with a soft, English, upper-class accent, spreads out the *draps*. No demarcation disputes, or sense of hierarchy among the staff, mar this production. If the director wants to move something, he moves it. The *décorateur* now works at lighting the thirty suspended lamps, filling them from a plastic bottle of Prior vegetable oil – a time-consuming job, as each lamp has five wicks. All the lamps sway slightly on their cords. Suddenly the whole scene becomes transformed into a magical cavern, flickering with mystery.

The actors have been rehearsing in an adjoining room. The Indian-Polish king of kings looks forward to the filming of 'The Game of Dice', for he feels that on stage it has always been unreal, and he could only achieve the right effect by an exaggerated emotional flourish. It had been difficult to avoid being childish . . . But now he can treat the whole illogical progression of the scene in an interior way, make the hero's springs of action more mysterious.

His antagonist, called Shakuni, is a powerful-looking Turkish actor, who, grey-bearded and with superb physical relish, plays the game as if it is a sexual contest. The scene begins with ceremonious greetings as the blind king – father of all the hundred Kauravas – and Gandhari, his blindfolded queen, enter to preside over the contest: 'For my blindness in the film,' says the veteran Grotowski actor, another Pole, who plays the king, 'I am just trying to react through my muscles.' The Vietnamese-born actress who plays Gandhari, in red robes of royalty, settles down to further sightless hours behind her bandages.

'On va répéter.' They run the scene. I edge forward to listen and look, and arrive at the border of the magic quilt. Shakuni bangs down his dice on the exquisite cross-shaped, dice-table. Yudhishthira challenges him:

> The powerful player who knows how to play and who ponders calmly is not worried by cheating. Here there is no crime, only the game, nothing but the game. A seasoned warrior fights against beginners, you call that cheating? Science is not cheating. You always enter a game with a wish to win. That's how life is. No cheat can ever defeat a master. Withdraw from the match if you are afraid.

A slippery reply, because Shakuni does cheat – or does he?

'Just a moment.' The director goes back to the beginning of the scene. 'I think what would be better . . . You all salute the king one by one . . . You all salute Shakuni . . . Everyone sits.'

The Japanese actor who plays the master of arms then asks, picking up a cushion, 'Can I move this?'

'No, you can't take it away . . . '

By this time, inadvertently, trying to eavesdrop on the interchange, I have strayed on to the sacred quilt – and have failed to remove my shoes. The director turns to me.

'This is a private rehearsal. Please be discreet,' he says, quite kindly, but with an edge of steel in his voice.

'Take off your shoes!' someone else barks out.

I withdraw in confusion. I know the director dislikes people intruding, and even in this very public setting I have failed to observe the invisible screens and barriers raised and lowered to protect the work. 'I hate letting people watch rehearsals because I believe that the work is privileged, thus private,' the director has written:

> There must be no concern about whether one is being foolish or making mistakes. Also a rehearsal may be incomprehensible – often excesses can be left or encouraged even to the amazement and dismay of the company until the moment is ripe to call a halt. But even in rehearsal there is a time when one needs outside people watching.

It has obviously not been the latter occasion. I resolve that this will be the only time I trespass on their territory. Of course, I know that nothing very world-shaking or remarkable has been said: that is not the point. The director continues with his quiet re-adjustments.

'The Game of Dice' continues all afternoon. Shooting this scene presents enormous problems of crescendo and diminuendo, so that Shakuni's 'I have won' never quite sounds right. Perhaps the scene has an overall problem in so far it is too much of a foregone conclusion – although the Polish actor catches beautifully the anguish of losing (and looks remarkably similar to the English Social Democrat leader, David Owen, while doing it). At one moment the designer remarks to me: 'It's funny how some people can sit and others will never be able to, whatever happens' – she refers to one of the minor characters.

In a previous scene Krishna, the god who intervenes in *The Mahabharata*'s action, tells Bhisma, son of the Ganges river goddess, that whatever he hears in the course of the game he must never interrupt. 'Wouldn't it be better to avoid the worst?' asks Bhisma. 'No,' says Krishna. 'Let each one go to his limit.'

But the director does intervene – quietly. He rearranges. He arbitrates. His is a different power of life and death. Where do his limits lie?

He calls '*Moteur*'. Once again, the filming starts.

Prior to being shot in Paris in 1988 as a six-hour film for television, and as a theatrical movie of about half that length, Peter Brook's nine-hour stage version of *The Mahabharata* was performed extensively throughout the world. This book, published to coincide with the television and film releases, has been devised as an authoritative celebration of the whole extraordinary event of *The Mahabharata*, from its beginning as a germ in the minds of two remarkable men – Peter Brook and his writer-collaborator Jean-Claude Carrière – through its stage performances in French and English, to its final transformation into moving pictures.

Work on the adaptation of the original Indian epic poem began as far back as 1974, when an eminent French Sanskrit scholar introduced Brook and Jean-Claude Carrière to stories from the ancient texts – originally dating from the middle of the first millennium B.C., although continuously added to in later centuries.

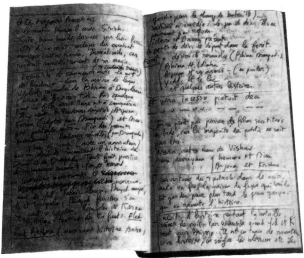

From Jean-Claude Carrière's *Mahabharata* notebook

Carrière explained the title: ' "*Maha*" in Sanskrit means "great" or "complete". A maharajah is a great king. "*Bharata*" is first of all the name of a legendary character, then that of a family or a clan. So the title can be understood as "The Great History of the *Bharatas*". But in an extended meaning, *Bharata* means Hindu, and even more generally, man. It can also be interpreted as "The Great History of Mankind".'

The Sanskrit texts consist of approximately 100,000 stanzas, making *The Mahabharata* – to quote the most usual comparisons – fifteen times longer than the Bible and eight times as long as *The Iliad* and *Odyssey* put together. As well as being an acknowledged masterpiece of Sanskrit literature, the poem contains thousands of beliefs, legends, teachings, thoughts and characters which are central to the Hindu tradition, and which are still part of everyday Indian life. Its centrepiece is the *Bhagavad Gita*, an extended conversation between Krishna and Arjuna on the battlefield before fighting begins, which reflects in particular the new perception of divinity which is often perceived as the basis of Hinduism today.

The cast of the two original stage productions, the first in French and the second in English, was based on the nucleus of performers from the experimental group with which Brook has worked in Paris since 1971, and represented twenty different countries, and a rich diversity of different styles of acting. Rehearsals of *The Mahabharata* began in Paris in September 1984 and continued for nine months, but even then the stage version had not reached its final form, and continued to be modified, or evolved further, long after its opening. Brook developed the performance along the lines of an improvisation – 'freeing the dynamic process', he called it – in the course of which arose confrontations and difficulties from the intense nature of the discipline demanded, and which, while fully expected, were not necessarily comfortable.

The Mahabharata first opened in July 1985 in a quarry near Avignon. From 1985 to 1987, in its French text, *The Mahabharata* toured Europe, with highly successful seasons in France, Greece, Italy, Germany, and Spain. In August 1987, with the English version of the play, the company embarked on an ambitious world tour which took it to Switzerland, the USA, Australia, Denmark, the UK, ending in July 1988 in Japan.

Wherever the production travelled it met with huge popularity and ecstatic acclaim. Every performance was sold out, and soon it became established as an artistic masterpiece and an international cultural event which transcended, in a unique and up to then unexplored way, the boundaries of race and creed. The nine-hour spectacle either played over three nights in its three parts ('The Game of Dice', 'Exile in the Forest', 'The War'), or in one continuous, marathon performance which lasted the whole day or, more frequently, the whole night. Thus, *The Mahabharata* reached and nourished three continents, a dozen countries, and some fifteen cities.

Production of the film in 1988 lasted fourteen weeks. As a property which defied ordinary definition and lay outside categories and rules, the film of *The Mahabharata* was shot not on video but on thirty-five millimetre. Brook described the six-hour film as the essence of the nine-hour story, but condensed, for ideas and action can be expressed on screen more quickly. 'I don't think anyone,' he said, 'will be able to tell what has been cut.'

Much has been recorded along *The Mahabharata*'s illustrious path. This book is an attempt to bring all the threads together and to render an account of the whole extraordinary phenomenon. It is based as much as possible on first-hand sources – including interviews with those taking part – and on my own observation of the filming, to which I was given complete access from September to December 1988.

I first met Brook in the mid-1960s when, on the strength of an interview, he recruited me as a member of the Royal Shakespeare Company at Stratford-upon-Avon, where I began to direct. This book has benefited enormously from Brook's generosity and willingness to talk to me. His example spread rapidly through the whole company, so that I can record with pleasure that I quickly became one of *The Mahabharata* family.

The Mahabharata bears supremely the stamp of one man's genius. Any book about the production must start with a description of Peter Brook's art and the position he holds as the outstanding theatrical innovator of our day. *The Mahabharata* is the peak of a life's effort to explore a vision of the theatre as a revitalising force to counter the decaying conventions of Western entertainment, which Brook has called 'The Deadly Theatre' – for example, the brutal warmth of Broadway, which he relates to 'the lack of emotional finesse . . . crude gestures of self-exposure . . . conditions where there is rarely the quiet and serenity in which anyone may expose himself'.

'What is not in *The Mahabharata*,' has been the comment of generations of Indian authors, 'is nowhere to be found . . .'

1

A corridor of echoes

Man is made by his belief. As he believes, so he is.

BHAGAVAD GITA

At the beginning of *The Mahabharata* the poet-narrator, whose name is Vyasa, announces to a child that he is going to tell him the history of his race: this is to be 'the poetical history of mankind'. Peter Brook has been a life-long Vyasa: he is acutely conscious that the theatre is a self-destructive, ephemeral art. The films he has made are – with the exceptions of *Lord of the Flies, Moderato Cantabile* and *Meetings with Remarkable Men* – the permanent records of his stage productions. All his work has this one element in common: it is essentially adaptation, re-telling. He invents the way of telling, but not that which, at a profound level, is being re-told. As Michael Birkett, his long-term film associate and friend, commented in 1988, 'Nothing much has changed about Peter. All artists are magpies. We seize upon what glitters.'

The Mahabharata's new Vyasa is a 'Gnome-like, short, tubby man in his 60s,' wrote an Indian journalist prior to this new adaptation's first production in July 1985, 'part Chaplin, part Rubinstein, with silver hair and twinkling blue eyes'. He was born on

Vyasa and the boy

29

March 21, 1925, in London, into a family of Russian-Jewish extraction. When only seventeen he began his theatrical career with an amateur production of Marlowe's *Doctor Faustus* at the Torch Theatre, London.

Brook's father, Simon, was born in Dvinsk in 1888 and was jailed for two months as a Menshevik before leaving Russia. He studied physics, mathematics, and electrical engineering at St Petersburg University. Brook's mother, Ida, was a chemistry graduate, also of St Petersburg. In the first world war she and Simon escaped as refugees to England where Simon became a pharmaceutical manufacturer and researcher – he patented the well-known laxative, Brooklax. They lived in Chiswick where Brook saw his first plays at the Chiswick Empire in the autumn of 1933, and owned his first 9.5mm cine-camera before the age of ten. He hated formal education, yet attended four preparatory schools. 'My anxious father withdrew me from one because the Head went mad, from another because the Head went bankrupt, from a third because the Head retired very suddenly, and from a fourth because the Head's wife left him . . . I highly approved of each successive calamity.'

His subsequent attendance at Westminster School was prematurely cut short by a glandular illness, the result of which is visible today in the scar on the right side of his neck. Aged twelve, Brook was dispatched with the swollen gland to Switzerland for a six-week nature cure, but in the sun his neck grew fatter and fatter, with an operation the inevitable outcome, and he had to remain in Switzerland for a total of eighteen months. He later discovered that the eminent doctor into whose care he had been committed had realised his whole life's work was misguided: but Brook had made good the gaps in his education by reading trashy fiction from Swiss convalescent libraries.

On his return home he spent an intensive spell at Gresham's School in Norfolk and then left full-time education to work in a unit making commercial and industrial films. In 1943 he tried to enter the secret service but the Medical Board would not grade him, so instead he went up to Oxford, to Magdalen College, where he read languages and had the good fortune to know C. S. Lewis, author of the Narnia children's books, and of *The Screwtape Letters*.

As President of the Oxford University Film Society, Brook made a film of Laurence Sterne's *A Sentimental Journey* and, as a result, was fined five pounds for neglecting his work: his father had to talk the Vice-President of his college out of sending him down. In 1944 he joined another film company. 'I want,' he said at the time, 'to be a vampire of the outside world and at intervals to give back the blood I have drawn out, in some creative form. I want to change and develop, and dread the thought of standing still.'

Brook's development by the age of twenty-four, when he had already made his first film, directed a dozen or so major theatrical productions, as well as four operas at Covent Garden – 'Opera is a nightmare of vast feuds over tiny details,' he said disgustedly – was decidely in an aesthetic direction. Kenneth Tynan described his appearance:

> Peter Brook is a small, sausage-shaped man: he looks edible, and one gets the notion that if one bit into him he would taste like fondant cream or preserved ginger . . . His miniature hands are limp, and flutteringly expressive: the rest of him stands quiet, dapper, casual and smug . . . His voice is flat and high-pitched, like a kazoo. One feels he has never travelled anywhere on foot or on buses, but is wrapped up in silk and carried.

But Tynan's description contained an element of deception. Brook was as tough as they came. 'In opera,' he confessed, 'there are so many people who fight with complete selfishness for their own point of view. Getting what you want is simply a matter of making the biggest fuss for the longest time . . . At an early age I learned to scream a little longer.'

There were intimations of his distant future development in his production of *Dark of the Moon* (1947), a folk-tale of religion and the supernatural set in the Smoky Mountains. In this he gave actors much greater scope for freedom and imagination than was current at the time. But the ascetic and scientific research director of a theatre with a laboratory idea – with strong paternal overtones – was a much later persona, the long and painfully difficult birth of which only just began as Brook approached the age of forty. (Brook dedicated his theatrical credo, *The Empty Space*, written in 1968, to his father.)

In 1950, with his production of *Ring Round the Moon*, Christopher Fry's adaptation of Jean Anouilh's *L'Invitation au château* in which Paul Scofield played the identical twin roles of Hugo and Frederick, Brook set the tone and style of his work for the next twelve years, until the turning-point of his production of *King Lear* in 1962 (his last stage production with Scofield, with whom he had first worked in Birmingham in 1945). This twelve-year period can be described as Brook's carefree, classical and literary period, during which the director took on little, if any, of the onus of having a vision, but was still prepared to be impish, shocking – somewhat an ageing *enfant terrible* by now – or purely captivating and entertaining. 'A theatre is like a violin,' he remarked. 'Its tone comes from its epoch and age, and tone is its most important quality.'

Extraordinarily enough, there are an astonishing number of

The Mahabharata

PETER BROOK'S EPIC IN THE MAKING

Below: Peter Brook and Michel Propper, the producer

Robert Langdon Lloyd (Vyasa)

Antonin Stahly-Vishwanadan (the boy)

Bruce Myers (Krishna)

Sotigui Kouyate (Bhisma)

Corinne Jaber (Amba)

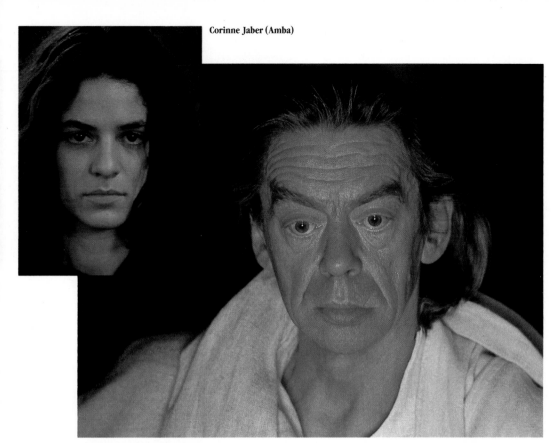

Ryszard Cieslak (Dhritharashtra)

Hélène Patarot (Gandhari)

Georges Corraface (Duryodhana)

Urs Bihler (Dushassana)

Miriam Goldschmidt (Kunti)

Erika Alexander (Madri/Hidimbi)

Jeffrey Kissoon (Karna)

Tapa Sudana (Pandu/Shiva/Salya)

Mamadou Dioumé (Bhima)

Andrzej Seweryn (Yudhishthira)

Vittorio Mezzogiorno
(Arjuna)

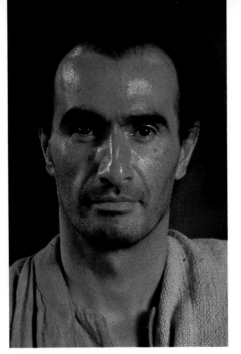

Mahmoud Tabrizi-Zadeh
(Sahadeva)

Jean-Paul Denizon (Nakula)

Mallika Sarabhai (Draupadi)

Yoshi Oida (Drona)

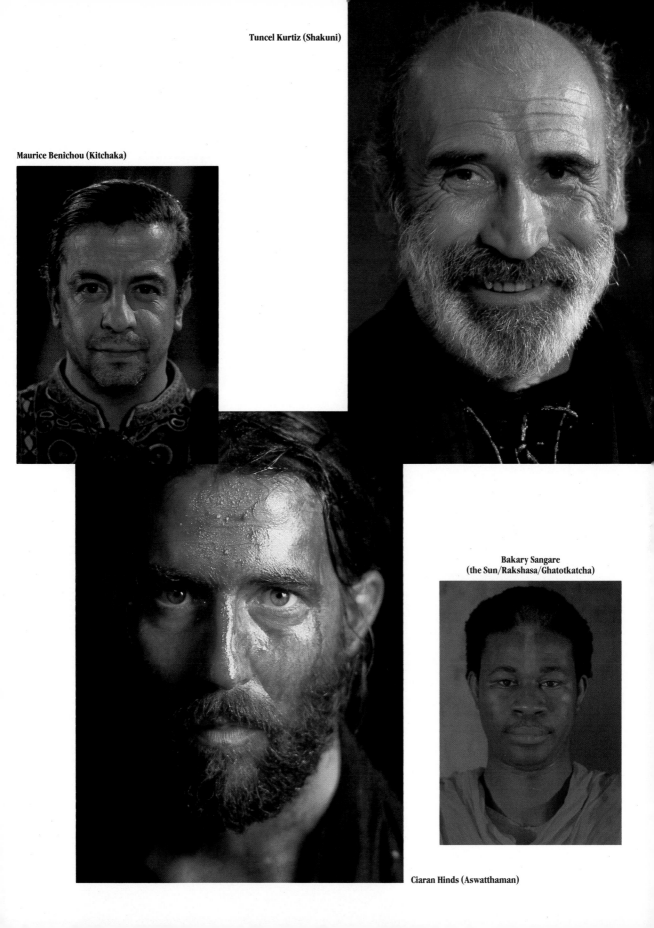

Tuncel Kurtiz (Shakuni)

Maurice Benichou (Kitchaka)

Bakary Sangare
(the Sun/Rakshasa/Ghatotkatcha)

Ciaran Hinds (Aswatthaman)

Left: Nolan Hemmings (Abhimanyu)

Below: Tamsir Niane (Urvasi)

Below: The Game of Dice

French plays directed by Brook during this time – not only more Anouilh, but at an even more popular level, André Roussin's *The Little Hut* which ran for three years and made Brook a small fortune, although he did not see eye to eye with Robert Morley, the star of the show. He also went on to direct the delightful musical *Irma la Douce*, and later – evidence of Brook's choice of plays turning to darker horses and becoming more eclectic – Jean Genet's lushly overwritten *The Balcony*, where action is transformed into symbolic ritual.

It is now forgotten that Brook was also the foremost directorial exponent of spiritual or Christian-orientated dramas: he not only directed Laurence Olivier as The Duke in Christopher Fry's *The Dark is Light Enough*, but also Graham Greene's *The Power and the Glory* and T. S. Eliot's *The Family Reunion*. Working with Olivier in *The Beggar's Opera* – and with Olivier and Vivien Leigh in the 1955–56 European tour of *Titus Andronicus* – confirmed that Brook could have little more to achieve by way of worldly success.

If there were distinguishing qualities in his productions at this time they were a lightness, a delicacy of touch, a kind of Chekhovian love of understatement, and a visual fastidiousness which often used extravagant means to begin with, and then cut them back ruthlessly. In *Titus* when Vivien Leigh as Lavinia had the awesome task of entering the stage after her rape and with her tongue cut out, Brook spared his audience the crude suggestiveness of realism. He simply half-veiled her face, while blood-red silk and red ribbon strands dangled from her shoulders to suggest the mutilation of her arms. The purpose of this was to give the audience as little as possible concrete outward realisation of the horror, but to stimulate their imaginations. 'If you stop regarding it as gratuitous melodrama and look instead for its completeness the play reveals its secrets,' Brook said.

In 1951 Brook married the dark-haired and pale-skinned Natasha Parry, a twenty-year-old beauty who had been one of Cochran's Young Ladies and who was described as having 'the tranquillity of a princess in a Persian miniature'. They both arrived ten minutes late for their wedding at Caxton Hall. Like Brook, Natasha is of Russian extraction, the daughter of a gambler and newspaperman, and through her mother related to Pushkin – but also a quarter Greek and a quarter English.

Their daughter, Irina, was born in 1962, and Simon, named after Brook's father, in 1965. Both children were christened in the Greek Orthodox Church. The Brooks travelled so much that Natasha commented, 'We came in hungry one evening to our Kensington cottage, and I said, "There are some sardines in a drawer in the kitchen." But there were not. They were in the drawer in the kitchen in our Paris flat. When you get muddles like that, it's time to settle down.' Natasha, who has a distinguished acting career, now lives in Paris, where Brook directed her in *The Cherry Orchard* early in 1981.

Up to 1962 Brook had dabbled in many styles, donned many different cloaks of magic, tapped impatiently with his wand and cast many, and even opposite, kinds of spell. At this point he seems to have decided that everything he had done up to then was not in any way a fulfilment, but the introductory experience necessary as a framework for beginning serious experiment.

He had, it is true, always had something of a wayward, unconventional approach, and has described how, when he came to direct his first big production of *Love's Labours Lost*, at Stratford in 1945, he agonised all night before the first rehearsal wondering how to 'block' the movements of the actors with forty pieces of cardboard and a model of the set. Next day when he started to move the actors according to his pre-set plan, he knew it would not work. 'They were not remotely like any cardboard figures, these large human beings thrusting themselves forward . . . We had only done the first stage of my movement, lettered A on my chart, but already everyone was wrongly placed and movement B could not follow. My heart sank.'

After a moment of panic in which he reflected on whether he should re-drill the actors, he gave in to the impulse to open himself to

Brook with 1st assistant Marc Guilbert

the pattern of the actors' movement which was unfolding in front of him. 'Rich in energy, full of personal variations, shaped by individual enthusiasms and laziness, promising such different rhythms, opening so many unexpected possibilities . . . I think, looking back, that my whole future work hung in the balance. I stopped, and walked away from my book, in amongst the actors. I have never looked at a written plan since.' After this production of *Love's Labours Lost* he was called 'a teddy-bear filled with dynamite'.

When he commenced rehearsing *King Lear* in early 1962 Brook had swung right round to thinking he wanted that unexpected element in a production to affect an audience as much as the actors; he now preferred the idea of what he called 'disturbance'. He said Lear was an assault on man's fatal blindness; and with this production he wanted to carry both his own idea of what the theatre was, and how the audience should be reacting, into an area of importance it did not have before. To achieve this, his approach grew into one of ruthless experiment. As Charles Marowitz, his assistant, wrote:

> He believes there is no such thing as the 'right way'.
> Every rehearsal dictates its own rhythm and its own state of completion. If what is wrong today is wrong tomorrow, tomorrow will reveal it, and it is through the constant elimination of possibilities that Brook finally arrives at interpretation.

At this early experimental stage Brook did not allow his audience the text's power of redemption, or any spiritual reassurance the catharsis at the end usually supplies. The plays of Samuel Beckett, in particular *Endgame*, had gained a strong hold over his imagination. Except in the wider Beckettian sense, he stripped *Lear* of its hopeful touches and made it pitilessly realistic, and in so doing cut against the values of much of the work he had directed in the previous ten years. To remove facile sentimentality, he denied Shakespeare his essential Christianity. He tore the remorse away from the men who put Gloucester's eyes out, and, in Tynan's judgment, dared to direct the play 'from a standpoint of moral neutrality'. But it could be argued that the morality was not totally neutral, and he was, as he said of Samuel Beckett, forging his 'merciless "no" out of a longing for "yes" and so his despair is the negative from which the contour of the opposite can be drawn'.

After *Lear* Brook went even further into the discontented, disaffected side of the human personality, taking on board the theories of two leading theatre theorists. The first of these was Jan Kott, whose influential *Shakespeare Our Contemporary* saw all the amoral cruelties of twentieth century politics and social life being worked out in Shakespeare's plays. Brook first met Kott in Warsaw in 1957, and some critics have claimed that his *Lear* was more influenced by Kott than by Beckett.

The second influence was that of the French experimental director, Antonin Artaud, whose vision of man was the opposite of

Echoes of *Endgame*

the organised 'thinking dust' that Paul Claudel glorified in his
theatrical output. Artaud subordinated the words of a text 'to the real
action', or, in other words, the symbolic gesture the actor was trying
to convey. It is this that Brook explored in the *Theatre of Cruelty*
experiment at London's Academy of Music and Dramatic Art in
1964. He was trying to find a discontinuous style of acting which
corresponded to daily life in the 1960s, which would free the
aggressive instincts, all too often trapped in the newspaper columns
or newsreel flashes, to roam freely on the stage.

Using Artaud more as a springboard than as a model for
re-creating Artaud's own world literally, Brook wanted to shock, to
make the audience confront itself, although, characteristically, he
justified this with the only absolute which he has consistently held
allegiance to all his life: the lasting superiority and greatness of
Shakespeare. For the 'cruelty' of Artaud, he claimed, was an effort to
recover the variety of Shakespeare's expression:

> Elizabethan theatre allows the dramatist space in which to move
> freely between the outer and the inner world. The strength and
> the miracle of Shakespearean texts lie in the fact that they
> present man simultaneously in all his aspects. We can in turn feel
> identified or take our distance, abandon ourselves to the illusion
> or refuse it; a primitive situation can disturb us in our
> subconscious, while our intelligence watches, comments,
> meditates.

It is perhaps hard to relate this search for complex consistency in the *Theatre of Cruelty* season to Charles Marowitz's Freudian and surrealist exploitation of *Hamlet*, or to Glenda Jackson's riveting and vulnerable undressing and bathing in the Christine Keeler sketch – one was arch and forced, the other much in the nature of a 'happening'. But there was much of this complexity evident in his production of *The Marat-Sade*, which occupied Brook largely during the rest of 1964, as well as during 1965 and 1966. The Shakespearean breadth of his interpretation of Peter Weiss's slanted Marxist play, which comes out on Brecht's rather than Artaud's side, pushed it towards universality of statement.

For this production Brook took expert advice from his brother Alexis, a consultant psychiatrist, visited asylums and studied paintings, applied all his directorial experience to date. According to Glenda Jackson, he believed that the only directing method to give results was a fusion of several different methods, all aimed at getting the actor to contribute more and more: every rehearsal became a living process. He worked closely with the actors, trying to get them to 'dig out the madman' from themselves. 'We were all convinced that we were going loony,' said Glenda Jackson. In fact he did not want to release the play from its rehearsal. With hindsight we can see that Brook perceived *The Marat-Sade* in his mind as a prototype of what he later achieved in *The Mahabharata*: as total theatre, using all the elements of the stage to serve the play –

> The strands of meaning of the play pass to and fro through its structure and the result is a very complex form: as in Genet, it is a hall of mirrors or a corridor of echoes – and one must keep looking front and back all the time to reach the author's sense.

One main difference, of course, between the productions of *The Marat-Sade* and *The Mahabharata* was that the first provided the excitement of clashing styles, and harsh or comically juxtaposed elements – it became a gaudy modern work for contemporary instruments – while *The Mahabharata* was a timeless distillation rooted in the past, but with a deep contemporary and spiritual relevance. But there was also a strong similarity: like *The Marat-Sade*, in which the lunatics break up their Charentan mad house, *The Mahabharata* has a violent – if more protracted and rationally sustained – ending.

By the time of *The Marat-Sade* three strands have clearly emerged in Brook's development as a director. The first is his taste for echoing images, which through successive works tend to become refined or developed further: failed ideas are never forgotten but stored away so they might come out years later. But these echoing

37

images are chosen or adapted to reinforce one central image of the play, what Brook calls its 'silhouette', and it is this that after the performance is over will remain with an audience. The second strand followed his, by now deeply confirmed, belief that the ultimate aim was always to find a contemporary density and complexity of style as rich as Shakespeare's. The third was the commitment to a wider realism in the theatre, into which all possibilities of approach, acting methods, and study had to be pressed.

U.S. (1966), filmed later as *Tell Me Lies*, caused very mixed reactions. The Lord Chamberlain telephoned the RSC chairman calling it 'bestial, anti-American, and Communist'; Irving Wardle, in *The Times*, called it 'vicarious psychodrama'; while the Bishop of Woolwich said it reminded him of Holy Week liturgy. In it Brook explored the American involvement in Vietnam, and certainly with a group of English actors tackling an American subject – and the unexpected participation of a new influence, the Polish theatre guru, Jerzy Grotowski – there seemed to be a dangerous swing to eclecticism, and even a precious element in some of the political posturings. Brook commented that the whole thing was a process, and a process can always 'go two ways, go forwards or go into reverse. Acting depends on bringing something all the time, otherwise it can turn in on itself and crumble.'

There was a tendency, perhaps, in *U.S.* to be inward-looking. Another of the problems with *U.S.* came from the pressure that, as part of the RSC's London enterprises, it was to run for five months at the large Aldwych Theatre. Brook would have preferred it to have had simply one performance.

But *U.S.* had presented a theme which later became very important in any consideration of *The Mahabharata*: it had asked the question that is continually at the centre of the discussion between Krishna and Arjuna in the *Bhagavad Gita* – whether to fight or not:

> *Arjuna*: My family will be massacred. If this is the price, who can
> wish for victory, or pleasure, or even life? Uncles, cousins,
> nephews and Drona, my teacher – they are all here. I can't bring
> death to my own family.

There was an increasing sense of desolation and restlessness in Brook's work between *U.S.* and the creation by Brook and the French producer, Micheline Rozan, late in 1970, of the Centre International de Récherches Théâtrales (CIRT) in Paris, when the urge to continue experiment within an increasingly structured framework triumphed over the appeal of glamorous presentations in the West End or on Broadway.

First of all he could not resist the attraction of working once

again with John Gielgud – with whom he had done *Measure for Measure* (1950) *Venice Preserved* (1953) and *The Tempest* (1957) – and he directed him in Seneca's *Oedipus* (1968) at the Old Vic. 'Gielgud,' he said, 'seems to have no method, which is in itself a method which has always worked wonders. His inconsistency is the truest of consistencies.' With much publicised improvisations and exercises, in which the older and more seasoned great actor participated eagerly with younger colleagues (with, especially, the elevation of the theatrical prop of the human phallus into something sacred and meaningful – as Colin Blakely, who played Creon, commented at the time, 'What it said to me was, you've just seen a load of cock') Brook was perhaps beating out a final tattoo on his *enfant terrible* drum. His former collaborator, Marowitz, observed 'Brook has gradually become the purveyor of avant-garde clichés to the mass audience. *Oedipus* is thinly disguised Open Theatre techniques, Grotowski tactics and lifts from *The Living Theatre*.'

Jean-Louis Barrault had invited Brook to come to Paris in May 1968 to form a Théâtre des Nations group working in private, an experiment prematurely curtailed by the student riots, but Brook's appetite for internationalism was stimulated further that year with his production, by a hybrid group of actors at London's Roundhouse, of a highly sexualised interpretation of *The Tempest* – 'fast and fluid sexual configurations,' wrote one critic – which culminated in Prospero's homosexual rape by his enslaved Island creatures. (Brook never thought of it this way.)

Brook may have been symbolising in this production his own discomfort with the role of director, which he wrote about in *The Empty Space*, also published in 1968: 'He does not ask to be God and

39

yet his role implies it. He wants to be fallible and yet an instinctive conspiracy of the actor is to make him the arbiter . . . In a sense the director is always an imposter, a guide at night who does not know the territory, and yet has no choice.'

Perhaps the composition of his group was as important for the future, and in particular for *The Mahabharata*, as the actual result itself. Although he had mixed actors from very different backgrounds in a previous production of Genet's *The Balcony* in Paris (1960), this was the first time, in a new awareness of how he wanted to proceed in the future, that Brook could observe the possible problems and benefits of mixing actors of different races. Two of that *Tempest* group, the Englishman, Bob Lloyd, and the Japanese, Yoshi Oida, were to become, much later, key performers in *The Mahabharata*.

Brook also gratified his search for adventure and his lust for travel, during this restless period, by filming *King Lear* in Jutland, Denmark, with Paul Scofield and most of the original cast reassembled some seven years after the stage production. As they could find only fairy-tale castles, they built their own dark age blockhouse in the middle of an icy wilderness: as Brook says, 'I don't believe in authenticity. I believe in conviction.' Over the Baltic water the great Russian director Grigori Kozintsev was shooting his own *King Lear*. Brook had only three months to film in, but Kozintsev had no such restrictions. 'How's it going?' the White Russian telegraphed his Communist counterpart: 'I think I finish never,' was the reply. The two directors exchanged packets of stills.

For the next four years Brook's fame, not only in his own country but also abroad, was held intact and was even expanded by the most successful production of his career, which remained unrivalled until *The Mahabharata*: his *A Midsummer Night's Dream*. With a revolutionary *coup de théâtre* he turned the magic inside out and set the whole play not in a fuzzy wonderland, but within the definite parameters of a circus. The idea was by no means new. Not only had Cocteau once conceived the idea, but not executed it – although he commissioned a score from Erik Satie – but Ariane Mnouchkine had directed *The Dream* in a circus ring in Montmartre, on a huge expanse of white fur. Calling the play 'the most savage and most violent piece that can be dreamed', she had made Titania's fairies appear like Red Indian chiefs – while Theseus resembled the Maharishi – although she had stopped short of Brook's leap into circus pyrotechnics.

'Aesthetic one-upmanship,' Marowitz called *The Dream*, scathing about the dislocation of its effects, but unappreciative of the deeper hold Brook had over the play, and his contact with Shakespeare's anonymous mind. At an acting level the text was superbly delivered and orchestrated in movement, and perhaps it was that very dislocation which, by the more universal image of the circus, transcended the rurality of the forest of Athens, freed the play and made it international in its appeal. It had both an appealing surface image and dense interior concentration. *A Midsummer Night's Dream* generated huge popularity, touring Canada and America, then Europe in 1972, while in the following year the production was dispatched with a largely different cast on a world tour.

With this umbrella, or circus canopy, spread over his enterprises, Brook could now successfully ally himself with his administrative collaborators and backers to give substance to his experimental dream. By no means was Brook the first director of the twentieth century to withdraw from popular success: *'L'insatisfaction m'inhabitait'* was the cry of Jacques Copeau, who, in 1920, deserted his thriving seasons at the Vieux-Colombier in a new search for the absolute. Copeau retired to Burgundy and formed a small touring company. Later, when this dispersed, he experimented with sacred drama in large open-air venues. He called this adaptation of medieval religious texts such as *Le Miracle du pain doré*, 'model sacred celebrations', and they expressed his ideal of a popular theatre of communion which blended both his spiritual aspirations and his passion to harness all the simple and direct expressive powers of the actor and his text.

Trapped in the iron disk *(Photograph by Sergei Obolensky)*

Brook's quest for the next fourteen years, although conducted with his own supreme form of showmanship, his cosmic charm, and manipulative wizardry, had a similar Copeauesque kernel. But – and this is his uniqueness – it was Brook's practicality, his grasp of the nature of the real world, and his ability to be in contact with, and relate to, other people which gave his vision not only its breadth but its possibility of attainment. Unlike other visionaries, Brook has never cut himself off to protect the uniqueness of what he saw, or sees: quite the reverse, he has systematically explored, with as much intimacy and openness as possible, all the major styles and revolutionary ideas which were available. Edward Gordon Craig, Stanislavski, Artaud, Grotowski, the Living Theatre, Joseph Chaikin's Open Theatre, have all been ingested, partly absorbed and partly rejected. Because his art ultimately resides in the power of selection, Brook has always been a great devourer – and an astute perceiver of the shortcomings of others. In a central revelation of *The Empty Space* he shows the process by which his mind works:

> The Living Theatre, exemplary in so many ways, has still not yet
> come to grips with its own essential dilemma. Searching for
> holiness without tradition, without sources, it is compelled to
> turn to many traditions, many sources – yoga, Zen,
> psychoanalysis, books, hearsay, discovery, inspiration – a rich
> but dangerous eclecticism. For the method that leads to what
> they are seeking cannot be an additive one. To subtract, to strip
> away can only be effected in the light of some constant. They are
> still in search of this constant.

If 'stripping away' was already established as Brook's main working method, 'the search for the constant' was to occupy him until September 1, 1984, when rehearsals began in Paris for the Avignon opening of *The Mahabharata*. The search was now firmly French based. It was hard, perhaps, to imagine an international centre of theatre research anywhere else dedicated exclusively to pushing forward the frontiers of a new kind of theatre, untrammelled by cultural or linguistic barriers. It is not being too cynically realistic to recognise that purses were more apt to fall open for scientific and serious-minded research: funds are rarely available for projects advertised as irreverent, anarchistic and wildly exciting.

Certainly it is hard to imagine such an enterprise beginning in England, which is, by its insular isolation, and the empiricism and opportunism of its people, not an internationally spirited community. Some of the aims of the centre were mixed up with the high-sounding mysticism which Brook often detonates around him to confuse sceptics and impress backers; a smoke-screen, perhaps, which allows him coolly to preserve his intentions and not to declare his hand until he is ready. But CIRT, first supported by international foundations, received a public subsidy from the French Government (by 1988 this had reached £400,000) and it led to the reopening of an old Paris theatre, Les Bouffes du Nord, in October 1974. This was the fruit of Brook's collaboration with Micheline Rozan, whose 'brilliance and originality of vision,' according to Brook, enabled him and his company, 'year after year, to cross the tightrope of survival'. The first production, Shakespeare's *Timon of Athens*, in a French version by Jean-Claude Carrière, was perhaps more French than international, but the work as a whole emerged as a masterpiece of simplicity which demonstrated that Brook had not, in any way, lost his touch.

The 'search for the constant' now proceeded slowly through long and arduous journeys and controversial experiments. The most important factor was that Brook had time to explore, without the pressure of having to show the public any finished performance until he was ready to do so. But he did ultimately stage his controversial experiments at festivals, and took them on limited tours.

The first of these was *Orghast at Persepolis* (1971), for which Ted Hughes contributed a melopoeic root language ('orghast') destined to strike deep at the heart of the unconscious. This enterprise smacked somewhat of the restless sophisticate's yearning for lost innocence, but when the work was performed in Iran, in the ruined palace of Darius the Great, under the auspices of the Peacock King, the *esprit Brooktien* triumphed again over disbelievers who might have raised the charge of pretentiousness. The late Richard Findlater made this observation on the whole *Orghast* experiment:

> There is, quite often, a noticeable element of wool in the verbal cloth of gold that shrouds what Brook says he is doing; but in what he does there shines out, repeatedly, the unmistakeable *mana* of the arch-magician, a self-renewing Prospero with enough of Puck in him to change his staff in time before it is snapped by theory.

Conference of the Birds (1973) saw, according to John Heilpern, who, as its chronicler, accompanied Brook and his international company into the heart of the Sahara desert, Brook losing his own identity, wiping the slate clean, and trying, as Heilpern said, 'to wake up on the other side of his identity'. I am not sure if this was so, preferring to believe that Brook was watching and waiting, trying out his many camouflages – one of which was the way he showed himself to Heilpern – and conflicting images. Perhaps the whole experiment was no more or less that of how actors from very different national and personal backgrounds could live together in a group. As Brook told Heilpern at another time:

It remains the one question every single person carries with him from the day he's born. How to live with other people? If you withdraw from life and become a hermit – in almost all cases you deprive yourself of everything you need the most. If you throw yourself into life the wrong way, you can easily find it swamps you. The formation of a real group is as difficult to achieve as the real identity of the people within it. I don't think there's any set of rules. Nor is any group structure a model or ideal. All one can say is that it's through this whole question of the individual versus society that a living community might evolve. The question can never be solved. But I think it can make a group come to life.

Possibly Heilpern's most accurate way of registering the mood of the whole trip remained in his amazement that 'throughout that long journey in search of truth and light, no issue managed to burn up quite so much nervous energy as the washing-up issue'. Frivolous perhaps, but a sign that the theatre – and theatre people – cannot wholly be divorced from reality.

There were other very positive aspects of *Conference of the Birds*. The fable of the birds' journey, taken from a twelfth century

Sufi poem, became partly based on the wordless playlets which Brook's troupe performed in African villages, and which they were forced to change with each different audience. They had to develop an openness to the childlike and natural response of the villagers, so they tapped what might be called, for want of a better term, archetypal dramatic roots.

Conference of the Birds also possessed a Shakespearean resonance which gave heart and commitment to the experimental ideal. The *Guardian*'s critic Michael Billington described how Brook the king of image-makers was still firmly in control. 'In *Conference of the Birds* when the birds reached the land of the Simorgh (their true king), the actors raised a group of bamboo poles from a fixed point on the floor to create a sense of a slowly opening chasm; the actors then gripped the poles horizontally and raised and lowered them at different speeds to create a kingdom filled with mirrors.'

The continuing quest for the constant – what we might call 'the perennial thread' – still fluctuated through what many commentators saw as the nadir of Brook's experimental period, and its most despairing message. *The Ik* (1975) presented a breakdown of family life, love and friendship and seemed to demonstrate that the Darwinian survival of the fittest had crushed the better side of humanity. *The Ik* displayed a broken world in which the wreckage was so clear, the silhouette so sharp, that, as Brook said, 'it seems to draw out for us very vividly how life once was, in the good times'.

Meetings with Remarkable Men (1977), a film based on G. I. Gurdjieff's book, took the need to fill the spiritual vacuum to further extremes, while Brook's stunning return to fulfil his need for popularity – the 'showman' as opposed to 'shaman' side of his personality – exploded with three different versions of Bizet's opera *Carmen*; with Alfred Jarry's *Ubu*; and with a timeless distillation of Chekhov's *The Cherry Orchard*, played first in French, later in English. By now the work of Brook's CIRT group, renamed the Centre International de Créations Théâtrales (CICT) had turned from laboratory into production line (with echoes of his father's pharmaceutical firm). After years in the wilderness it now had a solid base in Paris, and a gratifying demand for its appearances at every kind of international theatre conference or festival: revivals of the best work increased in frequency.

Speaking of *The Cherry Orchard*, before its Paris opening in 1981, Brook claimed that he was absolutely convinced that, in the white heat of writing, 'A playwright is dealing with the mysterious, almost formless, movement of human relationships which express themselves eventually through things said,' and that every great play 'is a skein of dialogue, a structure of tensions built out of phrases exchanged in the heat of the moment between human beings'. By this time preparatory work had started with Jean-Claude Carrière and the French Sanskrit scholar Philippe Lavastine on *The Mahabharata*. The quest that Brook had begun in 1970 had led him to place greater emphasis on that 'mysterious, almost formless, movement of human relationships' – the spiritual content of the play.

2

Lying is the number one sin

If I knew how to omit, I should ask no other knowledge.
R. L. STEVENSON

There is little or no doubt that Peter Brook and Jean-Claude Carrière, adaptor and playwright of *The Mahabharata,* had their timing right. Carrière even went as far as to say that his work on the play owed much to new forms of film screening, particularly the circle vision of La Géode at La Villette in Paris, where the film is not framed but spills over into reality. He cited an example shown recently when a film started conventionally, then the screen caught on fire, then a man appeared in the flesh on the stage to make an announcement, then you realised he was part of the film . . .

Carrière and Brook first worked together in 1973 when Carrière wrote the version of *Timon of Athens* which Brook directed for the opening of the Bouffes du Nord (Carrière's first play had been produced by Micheline Rozan in 1968). He and Brook have always been trying to broaden the vision, enlarge the theatre space. The Bouffes du Nord was a 'two-room' (auditorium and stage) theatre and 'we go towards a one-room theatre'. Carrière despised explanations, 'If you swim in your personal river you can't try to go back and swim backwards. I want to be in the river. I don't want to know what composes the river.'

'People are like rivers,' Tolstoy once wrote, 'they all contain the same water everywhere, yet each river at times can be narrow, swift, broad, smooth-flowing, clear, muddy, warm. So it is with people. Each man carries within himself the germs of all human qualities.'

Carrière loves the river image, particularly applicable as it is to *The Mahabharata.* One of Carrière's first and most powerful images as a child was of Sabu the Elephant boy, powerful and full of confidence, riding on the back of a snake in a deep river. He identified *The Mahabharata* with that image of Sabu's snake and saw Peter Brook next to him on the snake's back, leading the snake dance.

But to adapt the image – and Carrière's flexible and humorous mind delights in twists and turns of imagery – his first and most obvious observation about *The Mahabharata*'s director was that 'He is a brook. He's clear water, as clear as his eyes are revealing the grounds he goes through; he fertilises the grounds without floods, without violence. He will never stop. The brook has become a river –

it's Peter River. One day he will join the ocean.'

It is a striking feature of Western culture today that it will, in a way not seen since the huge materialistic expansion of the Roman Empire, accept Eastern religious fables and practices. The Hare Krishna cult, known as the International Society for Krishna Consciousness, was founded in 1966 by Swami Prabhupada and has its headquarters in Los Angeles. Youths of both sexes from non-Hindu backgrounds wearing dhotis and saris, and performing devotional songs, and dances, have been a feature of Western capital cities through the last decades.

With the weakening of traditional forms of Christianity, the exotic cults have offered a strangeness of appeal that has allowed people to embrace their rich trappings without necessarily penetrating to any profound identification with their deeper spiritual content. This superficial preference was well conveyed by a reviewer of *The Mahabharata* who wrote in the *Guardian,* '*The Mahabharata* is possibly the wisest story ever written – a vast epic of war and peace in India 2,000 years ago, fifteen times as long as the Bible, and so subtle and humorous in its perspective that it makes our own great religious epic look like a slim, grim, patriarchal episode in a more beautiful and many-layered story.'

Carrière in his house in Pigalle

In France Jean-Claude Carrière has earned the nickname of 'Griot', which is the special African caste entrusted with oral story-telling – 'Le Griot des Temps Modernes', the magazine *Rolling Stone* dubbed him. Born in the Hérault department of south France in 1931, he has varied his career remarkably. With a Ph.D in history, Carrière has a distinguished list of screen-writing credits, which includes six of Luis Buñuel's most famous feature films (including *Belle de jour* and *The Discreet Charm of the Bourgeoisie*). He wrote the screen plays for Milos Forman's *Taking Off*, Volker Schlöndorff's *The Tin Drum*, Daniel Vigne's *The Return of Martin Guerre* and Philip Kaufman's *The Unbearable Lightness of Being*.

He is a precise, serious writer, with a ruthless eye for the revision and condensation necessary for good film writing, and a gift for impersonality which makes him able to collaborate fully in a shared vision. Nothing of himself would apparently want to intrude, to become didactic or impose a style. 'Schéhérazade,' he says, 'is the patron saint of authors. She risks her life if she cannot command absolute power of attention. The voice of the story-teller must never be interrupted.'

He also had wide experience of the theatre before he began on *The Mahabharata*. His French adaptation of *Harold and Maude* (1973), in which I saw Madeleine Renaud play Maude with trance-like sublimity, was based on the film script of Colin Higgins's story about a young man of nineteen who wants to marry an old lady of seventy-nine. Carrière also adapted Tom Stoppard's *The Real Thing* in 1987 for the Paris stage.

It was, again, through Jean-Louis Barrault that Brook met Carrière in 1968. Later, when CIRT opened, Carrière went along to the Gobelins to watch the work of Brook: at this time all Brook had to rehearse in was a warehouse – a large white box 130 by 35 feet. 'Why,' Carrière asked himself, 'had this man, at the summit of his glory, who had worked with the greatest actors, never known anything but success – why had he installed himself in a place which was not even a theatre?'

To his adaptation of *Timon of Athens*, Carrière, by his judicious and highly selective use of vocabulary, brought an immediacy of feeling which appealed to Brook. In the tradition of Corneille and Racine, Carrière has a very definite and restricted theory of 'diction', which, while not so high-flown and poetic, he operates just as precisely. Brook saw – and still sees – in Carrière a modern Elizabethan, capable both of that Shakespearean concentration he so admires, and the brutal, direct, and simple contemporaneity which, thanks to Carrière's surrealist training with Buñuel, retains a surprising and unexpected element.

The response to *Timon* was gratifying; according to the Brook scholar, David Williams, the young audience in one Paris school, the Lycée Montaigne, was convinced it was seeing a play by a modern writer. Carrière then became the house writer of CIRT and then CICT. According to most accounts he and Brook began thinking about *The Mahabharata* as a possible project in 1974, when the Professor of Sanskrit in Paris, Philippe Lavastine, began telling Brook and Carrière stories from *The Mahabharata*. Lavastine, who had once been a companion of Gurdjieff, was not only a 'Brahmin' but a brilliant story-teller himself. Brook described the impact that first night had on him:

> We began to understand why this was one of the greatest works of humanity, and how, like all great works, it is both far from us and very near. It contains the most profound expressions of Hindu thought, and yet for over 2,000 years it has penetrated so intimately into the daily life of India that for many millions of people the characters are eternally alive – as real as members of their own family.

He and Carrière at once made the commitment – standing in the rue St André des Arts at three a.m. – to find a way of 'sharing these stories with an audience in the West'.

Carrière and Brook returned frequently, perhaps twice a week, to Lavastine for the next six months, and Lavastine continued to regale them with stories from the Sanskrit. Carrière took copious notes of numerous episodes, none of which figures in the final version. After two years without having read *The Mahabharata* at all, Carrière wrote a first draft of the play. The main aim, he decided, was to find the oral tradition through which the epic had been created and transmitted.

Reading his first version, Brook and he decided to persevere with *The Mahabharata* and now to attack the problem seriously, so they both sat down to read, in their respective languages, translations of the original. From 1980 Carrière began his preliminary work for writing the play. His first acting script took two years to complete – it was ready for rehearsal in September 1984.

Like Brook, Carrière is a researcher: thorough, methodical, but entirely instinctive in the progress he makes. His French version of *Conference of the Birds* (1979) had been considered a superb piece of work, epic, universal in appeal, amusing, philosophical in its commentary on the original. *The Mahabharata* had to be closer to India than *Conference* had been to Persia: India had to be present at every point in his adaptation.

He began with the self-appointed task of re-reading vast quantities of French poetry and drama in order to formulate an approach and see what dangers had to be avoided. The language research took him, he said, much longer than the detailed preparation for *Conference,* and he was at first aware of the tremendous pitfalls of using as models both French classical tragedies, such as those of Racine, and romantic dramas such as those of Victor Hugo. Confrontation, conflict of character, rousing emotions – all this was eliminated right at the beginning.

There is very little French literature inspired by India, but a five-page poem from Victor Hugo's nineteenth century epic *La Légende des siècles* caught his attention because, almost uniquely, it had a Vedic theme. Perhaps more crucially to *The Mahabharata* scheme, Hugo had evolved a new form of epic in which no specific set of national gods or heroes was exclusively the subject, but mankind itself became the hero of the epic tale. This vital jump made Hugo highly eclectic in his choice of subjects for *La Légende des siècles,* and he ranges through human history in short and powerful poems, unified only by a ruling idea. Hugo's example and, in particular, a compelling atmosphere of Vedic mythology in the poem *Suprématie,* inspired Carrière and gave him a strong instinct as to how to proceed. Later, one of his first actions with the newly assembled cast was to read Hugo's poem aloud to them.

Perhaps it was Hugo's confidence which, above all, Carrière found helpful. *Suprématie* presents nakedly and clearly, without any nuance, an encounter taken from one of the Upanishads between Vayu, god of the wind, Agni, god of fire, Indra, god of space, and a mysterious light which 'has the eyes of a figure' – an enlightenment which then, by the clever use of a blade of straw, demonstrates to these three all powerful gods that their might is completely meaningless. The wind cannot blow away the straw, nor can fire burn it, and while Indra, the all-seeing and all-knowing, can view the straw, he cannot stop the light from disappearing from his omniscient eye.

This attempt to define man's inadequacy in describing the enlightenment, or true god, had impressed Hugo. *Suprématie* captures the relativity of any of man's invented deities, the limits of his knowledge of God – and therefore puts the Hindu figures into a Western perspective. It is this sense of unfinished formulation, of tentative seeking, of finding that one element is always contradicting and crossing out another, which permeates Carrière's final version of *The Mahabharata* with uncanny balance; in some respects it remains close to Hugo's vision of deities.

But Carrière found Hugo's own poetic practice hard to follow. His immediate temptation was to write *The Mahabharata* as Hugo would have written it – in verse. He tried verse but this seemed ridiculously pompous, although Hugo's own poem achieves at times a remarkable simplicity and directness. An element of this quality shines through Carrière's version, for example when Hugo writes of the three gods first meeting the light:

C'était un flamboiement immobile, pensif,
Debout. Et les trois dieux s'etonnèrent. Ils dirent:
'Qu'est ceci?' Tout se tut et les cieux attendirent.
'Dieu Vâyou, dit Agni, dieu Vâyou, dit Indra.
Parle à cette lumière. Elle te répondra.
Crois-tu que tu pourrais savoir ce qu'elle est?' – Certes,
Dit Vâyou. Je le puis.

It was a thoughtful and immobile flame,
An upright flame. And the three gods were struck with
          amazement. They said:
'What is this?' Everyone held his tongue and heaven waited.
'God Vayu, said Agni, God Vayu, said Indra.
Speak to that light. She will reply.
Is it possible to know what she is?' Of course,
Said Vayu. I will find out.

Carrière's next move was to proscribe all words which had a precise Western association: first Christian terms such as 'sin', 'soul', 'eternal life', 'redemption', 'incarnation'; next medieval words such as 'knight', 'suzerain' or 'principality'; then classical or neo-classical vocabulary; then nineteenth century 'Parnassian', pomposity – what he called, 'all the pseudo-antique words of Flaubert's *Salammbô* or of José-Maria de Hérédia.' Words, too, with twentieth-century Freudian echoes were forbidden – such as 'subconscious', 'unconscious', 'super-ego' and so on.

'I was very faithful to what happens in the real story,' Carrière insisted. 'I would never invent new sacred words. I'd be totally unable to. Many traditions in the world, not only the Indian but the Chinese and many others, say that lying is the number one sin. They feel that someone who steals or kills can be punished and corrected, but a liar endangers social relationships. That's why in *Measure for Measure,* for instance, the only person who is not pardoned at the end by the Duke is Lucio, because he is a liar. This gives an idea of the strength and power of words.'

Carrière gave as the best example of this – words having the weight of oaths – when the hunter is cursed by the dying gazelle he has shot. Another moment he cited was of Arjuna's arrival to tease Kunti, his mother, into guessing the prize he has won in a tournament. 'You must share everything with your brothers,' says Kunti almost as a reflex. 'But it's a woman,' Arjuna tells her. Because she cannot withdraw her words, Arjuna has to comply.

The vocabulary became very limited and very conscious. Carrière found himself doing as he had done in his versions of *Timon of Athens* and *Measure for Measure,* counting the repetition of words, and finding different levels or layers of words to give a different dimension. For instance the repetition of 'sun' and 'moon', 'dark' and 'light', would give a cosmic dimension, while 'friend', 'gold', 'thief', suggested something else. For *The Mahabharata* Carrière settled on five key words, all monosyllabic:

LIFE	VIE
BLOOD	SANG
HEART	COEUR
FIRE	FEU
END	FIN

These reverberated throughout the text, especially as Carrière then tried, within the constraints of this limited vocabulary, 'to put together words not usually put together'.

DHRITHARASHTRA: (*à Bhisma*) Ce monde est sauvage. Comment connaître la sauvagerie de ce monde?
BHISMA: Elle est autour de toi.
DHRITHARASHTRA: Comment lui échapper?
Bhisma se redresse
BHISMA: Un homme s'avance dans une forêt obscure et peuplée de bêtes féroces. La forêt est entourée par un immense filet. L'homme est touché par la peur, il court pour échapper aux fauves, il tombe dans un puits noir. Par un prodige il reste accroché à des herbes, à des racines enchevêtrées. Il sent le souffle chaud d'un énorme serpent qui ouvre sa gueule au fond du puits, il va tomber dans cette gueule, au bord du trou un éléphant gigantesque va l'écraser, des souris blanches et noires grignotent les racines auxquelles l'homme est pendu, des abeilles dangereuses volent au-dessus du trou, et laissent tomber des

gouttes de miel . . . Alors l'homme tend le doigt, doucement, avec précaution, il tend le doigt pour recueillir les gouttes de miel. Menacé par tant de dangers, au bord de tant de morts, il ne connaît pas l'indifférence, le goût du miel l'anime encore.

DHRITHARASHTRA: Et toi? As-tu encore envie de miel?

Bhisma ne répond pas.

DHRITHARASHTRA: Bhisma, répond-moi.

Bhisma ne répond pas. Il est mort. Sandjaya repose sa tête sur son oreiller de flèches.

SANDJAYA: Le souffle l'a quitté.

DHRITHARASHTRA: (*to Bhisma*) This world is savage. How can one understand the savagery of this world?

BHISMA: You are part of it.

DHRITHARASHTRA: How can one escape?

Bhisma draws himself up.

BHISMA: A man is walking in a dark, dangerous forest, filled with wild beasts. The forest is surrounded by a vast net. The man is afraid, he runs to escape from the beasts, he falls into a pitch-black hole. By a miracle, he is caught in some twisted roots. He feels the hot breath of an enormous snake, its jaws wide-open, lying at the bottom of the pit. He is about to fall into these jaws. On the edge of the hole, a huge elephant is about to crush him. Black and white mice gnaw the roots from which the man is hanging. Dangerous bees fly over the hole letting fall drops of honey . . . Then the man holds out his finger – slowly, cautiously – he holds out his finger to catch the drops of honey. Threatened by so many dangers, with hardly a breath between him and so many deaths, he still has not reached indifference. The thought of honey holds him to life.

DHRITHARASHTRA: And you? Do you still wish for honey?

Bhisma does not reply. Bhisma answer me. *Bhisma does not reply. He is dead. Sandjaya rests his head on a pillow of arrows.*

SANDJAYA: His breath has left him.

(*Translated by Peter Brook*)

The only son of a '*petit viticulteur taciturne*', Carrière grew up in a house without books. He recalled that at the age of five he asked his mother for a Buddha as a Christmas present. His parents did not know what it was, and went to ask the country *curé*, who was not any the wiser but gave his agreement. In the bazaar of Bédarieux his mother found a gold-plated Buddha which he has to this day.

He claimed that *The Mahabharata* was the show 'that I wanted to watch since I was a little boy' and that he had seen it sixty times, having travelled to view it in Los Angeles, New York, Copenhagen, Glasgow and Zürich as well as, of course, at Avignon and the Bouffes du Nord in Paris. He preferred the adaptation to his own original plays.

Carrière visited India to gather all kinds of images and impressions – 'Images of dance, film, marionette theatre, village celebrations and plays'. Brook rejected the images from the Kathakali, the classic dance drama of Kerala, Southern India, in their playing of *The Mahabharata,* for being too visually closed and finite, too stylised. It seemed to have nothing to do with his own life. However, there must have been stylistic qualities which influenced him and Carrière. I recall, from the Kathakali's four-hour version of *The Mahabharata,* played in Paris, particularly the oil flame burning on stage all the time: a kind of *lumière protectrice* (protective light) to the actors who allowed themselves to be possessed of the dangerous spirits of the characters they impersonated. Another element which Brook may have incorporated was the way – common not only to Kathakali but Brook productions as a whole – colours signified a quality. Green, for instance, with a white border of rice paste was for gods and divine heroes.

Most of all the hand gestures had impressed me: heightened by

Jean-Claude Carrière's snapshots of India

silver nail-tips the hands wove, flashed and echoed every form of human and divine state. Imitative, descriptive and symbolic in turn, they played 'The Game of Dice' exquisitely as high farce.

Brook summarised eloquently the overall impact on them of the Indian way of life – again employing the image of the river:

> We saw that for several thousand years India has lived in a climate of constant creativity. Even if life flows with the majestic slowness of a great river, at the same time, within the current, each atom has its own dynamic energy. Whatever the aspect of human experience, the Indian has indefatigably explored every possibility. If it is that most humble and most amazing of human instruments, a finger, everything that a finger can do has been explored and codified. If it is a word, a breath, a limb, a sound, a note – or a stone or a colour or a cloth – all its aspects, practical artistic and spiritual, have been investigated and linked together. The line between performance and ceremony is hard to draw, and we witnessed many events that took us close to Vedic times, or close to the energy that is uniquely Indian.

Carrière sketched and took voluminous notes. He observed, together with the cast, that, in India, no religious idea had ever died and been superseded. Everything was still there, omnipresent, and Hindu mystical thought, uninhibited by dogma, had remained wondrously complex and rich (in another word, Shakespearean). Particularly appealing to him was how it seemed a laboratory for understanding the strivings of the religious mind. There was no aspect of Hindu life that was not entwined in mythology. Wherever people found themselves, they would participate in dramatisations of cosmic divine events: as Carrière said, 'They dare to be Krishna – and even Shiva' – while in the temples the different icons demonstrated the feats of a wide variety of gods. According to *The Mahabharata* there are 33,333 Hindu deities. Without meeting all of them the visitors participated in a wide range of ceremonies.

This freed Carrière's imagination rather than closing it down: the constant sense of improvisation, of change, made him realise that the form of *The Mahabharata* was not steady but constantly on the move. He felt obliged to invent scenes, such as the meeting between Krishna and Bhisma in which Krishna instructs the celibate king not to intervene in the game of dice. This gave Carrière the chance to clarify the notion of *dharma,* the understanding of which is crucial to the whole understanding of *The Mahabharata.* The encyclopaedic definition is 'the complex of supernaturally sanctioned moral, social,

Drawings of India from Carrière's notebook

and ritual laws, which are incumbent upon an individual according to his station in life'. Aldous Huxley defined two forms of *dharma* in *The Perennial Philosophy*:

> The *dharma* of an individual is, first of all, his essential nature, the intrinsic law of his being and development. But *dharma* also signifies the law of righteousness and piety. The implications of this double meaning are clear: a man's duty, how he ought to live, what he ought to believe and what he ought to do about his beliefs – these things are conditioned by his essential nature, his constitution and temperament. Going a good deal further than do the Catholics, with their doctrine of vocations, the Indians admit the right of individuals with different *dharmas* to worship different aspects or conceptions of the divine. Hence the almost total absence, among Hindus and Buddhists, of bloody persecutions, religious wars and proselytizing imperialism.

The story of *The Mahabharata* might appear to contradict the latter part of that statement, but Carrière's definition of *dharma*, a word which is left in its original throughout the play, is close to Huxley's. '*Dharma* is the law on which rests the order of the world,' he wrote in his introduction to the printed edition of the play. '*Dharma* is also the personal and secret order each human being recognizes as his own, the law he must obey. And the *dharma* of the individual, if it is respected, is the warrant of its faithful reflection of a cosmic order.'

The decline and destruction of *dharma* in the world is the *sine*

The poisoned lake of Dharma

qua non of the play of *The Mahabharata* and the reason why Krishna descends on earth with his superior tricks to restore it. As the central narrative unfolds, that of the long and bloody quarrel between the Pandavas, the five hero-brothers 'pressed by the will of the gods', and the Kauravas, their cousins, of whom there were a hundred, what emerges is a highly fatalistic view of destruction visited on men by the gods. The ever-worsening moral and physical conflicts, in what is at heart a family battle, culminate in a terrible war of annihilation where, by implication, the fate of the whole world is at stake.

In the face of these conflicts the story depicts a great range of human response; one character may acquiesce bravely in the fate he has to meet; another strives to impose his will over that of the gods; a third may act blindly, not knowing who he is; a fourth may follow an impartial code – that of goodness or military honour. The story may be understood as the moment when men cut the strings that tie them to the gods, becoming human with all the problems that have plagued the world since its origins. To save *dharma*, Krishna induces the Pandavas to conduct the war, when fair means prove inadequate, with guile and trickery.

'I believe that this is one of the deepest themes and certainly the one that touches me most,' said Carrière. 'As Vyasa voices it at the beginning, I have written this poem to inscribe *dharma* in the hearts of men.' Carrière added, 'And I hope it was my *dharma* to write *The Mahabharata!*'

Carrière made it clear that nearly half the scenes in the play do not exist in the original. He had cut the secondary stories – which are those the characters tell among themselves – but reinforced and filled out the principal events, finding different ways of enriching the sixteen main personages by incorporating in them bits of other abandoned characters. The didactic matter had also been cut, for instance the 300 pages when Bhisma as he lies dying expounds on the duties of the king and how society should be organised.

At the end of the play Carrière condensed the thirty-six years and all the adventures that take place after the war into three scenes: the death of Krishna (whom he kept deliberately ambiguous in his nature of man or god, preserving his two faces, and emphasising 'their opposite and paradoxical nature'); the death of the blind King Dhritharashtra and his wife, Kunti, on the river bank (in the original it says that they went towards the forest), and the ending with everyone in Paradise. 'That installation' Carrière called it, 'of all the characters in the peace of a world where everyone has found his place; that final repose when the actors talk among themselves, contemplate each other and listen to the music – the "final what every one makes of himself" – I regard as the most beautiful ending in the theatre I have ever seen.'

'Man or God? It is not up to us to decide,' Carrière had written about Krishna. John D. Smith, the Cambridge Sanskrit scholar disagreed in the English *Times Literary Supplement*:

> That Krishna is a paradoxical figure is beyond dispute – so are other Hindu gods, notably Shiva and the Goddess – and he is certainly the most human of the deities. But Carrière is simply not correct when he says that 'in *The Mahabharata,* at least in those parts of the poem generally thought to be the earliest, nothing clearly indicates that he is an avatar, one of the earthly incarnations of Vishnu'. *Mahabharata* 5.22 is a chapter that can be shown on internal (metrical) evidence to be uniformly early: at Stanza 10 Krishna is referred to as 'Vishnu the unassailable, the great overlord of the three worlds'. Unlike *The Ramayana,* the other great Sanskrit epic, *The Mahabharata* acknowledges its central god's identity with Vishnu from the start.

Smith continued in his review that, in the difficult choices about what to include and what to omit, Carrière and Brook's decisions otherwise make excellent sense: 'minor simplifications are made in the involved domestic history which leads up to the war, and in the conduct of the war itself, with no ill effects for the overall narrative.

A single unfortunate omission is Bhima's vow to break Duryodhana's thigh, made after Duryodhana insults the heroes' joint wife Draupadi by baring his thigh at her, and paralleled by Bhima's vow to drink Dushassana's blood to avenge another similar insult. Both insults are included in the play, as are both of Bhima's terrible deeds, so it seems a pity to have lost the thread of motivation in one case.' (This was rectified in the screen version.)

But 'Is it the *Mahabharata*?' asked the authoritative John Smith. His answer was a resounding 'Yes' – the adaptation was remarkably faithful to the events, 'sometimes even the wording, of the Sanskrit original'. More important, it was true to its spirit. 'This is not "Peter Brook's *Mahabharata*"; this is the Indian epic *Mahabharata*, lovingly cast by Brook into a form which non-Indian audiences can share.'

Other critics did feel that there was quite a lot of occidental opportunism in Carrière's text of *The Mahabharata;* that it conceals cynicism in its refusal to find hope or any answer; that, too, it is a worldly work which supplies the flavour of religion without the commitment. The *Sunday Times* critic, John Peter, quoted Nirad Chaudhuri – 'Hinduism is about power', and described how the characters were bent on holding power and avenging any attempt to take it away: this amoral tale, claimed Peter, had been cast into an essentially moral form yet without any moral conclusion:

> Yudhishthira loses his kingdom in a game of dice, but he can't explain why he played in the first place. 'Victory and defeat, pleasure and pain,' the princes are told, 'are all the same. Act but don't think about the consequences of your actions.' Strictly speaking, this is incomprehensible to the Western mind. In *The Mahabharata*'s Paradise, good and evil are cancelled in a strangely touching atmosphere of resignation and pride. Pain is not forgotten; it is absorbed and transcended. This has nothing to do with our ideas of forgiveness or maturity. A lot of people have suffered and died, but morally speaking nothing has happened. One side possesses a 'limitless weapon' which could destroy the whole world. We squirm uncomfortably with the relevance of this, but the subject isn't developed: the quarrel is finally ended by butchery.

But if Peter reacted at the level of *The Mahabharata*'s strength or weakness of morality, and questioned its premises, the more general reaction was to applaud Carrière's art of story-telling. For instance Michel Cournot, in *Le Monde,* called the French version a 'fairy tale which spoke to each of us intimately . . . Everything speaks directly to the five senses and finds its way to the soul.' My own view is that Carrière and Brook achieved the necessary 'willing suspension of disbelief' in their adaptation. They also, and perhaps more crucially, managed a suspension of moral evaluation, while supplying hints and possibilities of this. The characters are changing all the time and one is continually kept guessing as to how the consequences of their actions will affect themselves and each other. The whole work becomes narrative based not so much on events to be taken morally and literally, but mythologically and magically, in terms of how this narrative is evoked. From a moral point of view *The Mahabharata* seems to have had its cake and eaten it.

Would you like to eat ?

AMBA
I only eat what the wind brings. I never sleep. All my life I walk and question. I need nothing.

She walks defiantly away, into the marshes. The brothers return to their occupations, but DRAUPADI is deeply affected by the meeting with AMBA.

DRAUPADI
Someone is laughing at us.

YUDHISHTIRA
What are you saying ?

DRAUPADI
A magician had made us blind, he's torturing us.

YUDHISHTIRA
What magician ?

The other brothers have ceased all activity. They listen motionless, heads bowed.

DRAUPADI
I was dragged in front of everyone clothed in a single robe, stained with my blood. My husbands were there, I had given each of them a son, I needed their aid and Duryodhana is still alive ! I despise your strength.

No one answers her. She adds:

I have another question.

YUDHISHTIRA raises his eyes and watches her.

A page of the film script

'Our production of *The Mahabharata* is proof that theatre really can convey everything,' averred Carrière, who did not cease being involved once he had completed his script. He continued his modifications right up until the first night at Avignon – and beyond.

Even when *The Mahabharata* opened Carrière was still constantly involved both in the planning and in the writing of the screenplay, in the translation into English, in ceaseless interviews and in critical reappraisals he himself made of the production. By this process, and by the testing of the scenes in rehearsal, Carrière found the structure of his script, with its strengths and its weaknesses, pitilessly exposed. 'It forced on you a completely honest work where no intellectual argument will protect you, no fancy writing can trick you. True direction is not the way the actors move, the decors and the lights,' he said. 'True production is invisible.'

Carrière emphasised continually that the form of *The Mahabharata* was not fixed or steady; the fact that his new additions of scenes were being translated into Hindi confirmed the work's enormity, its generosity, and its welcoming quality. He felt honoured to have brought a few new details to the epic and to have explored the truth that we are all, deep down, individually responsible for the universe. He rejoiced in its flexibility and its ability to renew itself: he boasted 'I can tell you the story of *The Mahabharata* in one phrase.'

'In Avignon,' Carrière expostulated with pride, '25,000 tickets sold and 60,000 people were turned away: in spite of this the movie people were saying, "It's not popular".'

Carrière has two shelves in his Pigalle house lined with *The Mahabharata,* and boxes filled with the 15,000 or more pages of work he himself put into it. 'One of the many, many lessons of *The Mahabharata* is that the obvious things are incomprehensible.' So, too, was how the project all came together. 'I know a very small line of water in a meadow in Bavaria, almost hidden by the grass. It is called the origin. This is one of several sources, several brooklets. If you go barefoot walking up the grass you get healed – so many people come here and they go walking very slowly,' he said. 'At one point all the sources have to come together and make one – or if they go to different sides of the mountain they get lost. The forces of self-destruction are as strong as self-healing.'

The quarry at Avignon

THE GAME OF DICE

Vyasa starts to tell the child the story of his race

Bhisma contemplates the problem of life-long celibacy

The story-teller begets the characters

Pandu hunting the amorous gazelle

Kunti's mantra

Gandhari's wedding

**Above: Gandhari giving birth to a hundred sons
- the Kauravas**

Above: Pandu dies because he cannot resist the charms of Madri

Drona's arrival

Above: Draupadi about to marry the five brothers

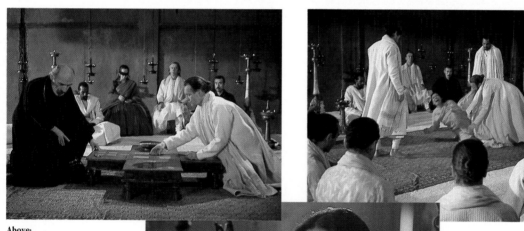

**Above:
Yudhishthira
losing the
game**

**Right:
Draupadi fears
the worst**

**Above:
Dushassana
enslaves her**

EXILE IN THE FOREST

The Pandavas
in exile

Below: Amba in search of Bhisma

The mothers meet

Bhima watching

The Kauravas evoke Arjuna by magic

Arjuna in the mountains

Arjuna appears

The fight

Karna seeks the absolute weapon

Virata's court

Draupadi disguised as a serving girl

Catching Kitchaka's eye

THE WAR

Above: the Bhagavad Gita

Below: the first battle

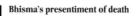
Bhisma's presentiment of death

The last fight

Abhimanyu in Drona's iron disk

Draupadi mourns the
death of Abhimanyu

Ghatotkatcha about to be
slain by Karna's magic lance

Drona covers himself in blood before his execution

Bhima and Dushassana fighting

Draupadi washing her hair in Dushassana's blood

Krishna and Arjuna

Duryodhana hides in the icy lake

Duryodhana meets Bhima

Bhisma on his death litter

Krishna killed by a hunter

Paradise

3

The rim of the universe

We are not the personal creators of our truths, but
only their exponents who thus make articulate
the psychic needs of our day.

CARL JUNG

After dress rehearsal at the Bouffes du Nord in August 1987, the English *Mahabharata* had set out for its year-long world tour, during which it visited eight cities in three continents. The French version, confined to Europe, had enjoyed a huge success and reputation, but this was a completely new beginning. One of the most important characters, Vyasa, had been cast at only the last moment: Bob Lloyd suddenly found himself with only four and a half weeks rehearsal. Fortunately he could draw on his long-term experience of working with Brook, although in the short-term he had no one to rehearse with – everyone was on holiday – and he developed a raging toothache. At his first performance, Lloyd said, 'The story-teller was the only one who didn't know what was happening!'

British critics who travelled to Zürich for the English language première lamented its absence from their native shores: there had been much-publicised talk of performing it in London's Docklands. But the enterprising Mayor of Zürich had stepped in with generous backing for the short run of a week, and the Swiss had flooded in their thousands to the boat-house by the edge of the Zürichsee.

There were gains as well as losses in seeing it performed inside in English, rather than outdoors at Avignon in French. The gain was, according to Michael Billington, 'a greater intimacy and a realisation that Brook's production is a superlative piece of narrative theatre that seems like a summation of all that he has learned.' The loss was that of the landscape, lyrically described by Michael Ratcliffe of the *Observer* two years earlier at Avignon.

White dust and the scent of lavender and thyme fill the evening air on the walk up from the river; pines, cypresses, vineyards and olives fill the valley below. Cables are looped over the *maquis* from a generator beside the path; police and *pompiers* stand on call further down, staring at the pilgrims in phlegmatic disbelief. . . . From a defile high in the rock the piercing and giddy fanfare of a nagaswaram announces the approach of the first play. The nagaswaram is a shawm-like instrument which, half-trumpet, half-pipe, produces a wild and thrilling sound, sometimes ceremonial, sometimes in grief. When the long notes stop, they do so with dramatic abruptness and reveal the acoustic of the quarry to be without echo of any kind: fine, dry, clear.

There was the loss, too, of Carrière's original French version, considered better from a literary point of view: 'French scholars tell me they miss in English the mystical quality of French prose known as "*l'hindouisme*". In compensation English has more sinew as a theatrical language.' (Billington.)

Lloyd felt 'like an obvious sore thumb' in Zürich, but he developed then and there a secondary relationship with *The Mahabharata* which lasted him until the end of the tour – that of watching it from the wings when he was not on stage. He became so happy thus engaged that he had, he said, 'to pinch myself to believe I am seeing what I am seeing – this is not a dream, this is as real as real can be.' He then found that he had to act worried in order to go back on stage. Miriam Goldschmidt (Kunti) told me how Brook joked with them in Zürich: 'Please don't be too proud. They paid a lot of money for this.'

MAHABHARATA
EIN INDISCHES EPOS IN DREI TEILEN
WELTPREMIERE DER ENGLISCHEN VERSION
ADAPTATION: JEAN-CLAUDE CARRIERE
DEKOR UND KOSTÜME: CHLOE OBOLENSKY
INSZENIERUNG:

PETER BROOK

COPRODUKTION:
CENTRE INTERNATIONAL DE CRÉATIONS THÉÂTRALES, PARIS
ROYAL SHAKESPEARE THEATRE, LONDON
BROOKLIN ACADEMY OF MUSIC, NEW YORK
AUSTRALIAN BICENTENNIAL AUTHORITY, SYDNEY
PRÄSIDIALABTEILUNG, ZÜRICH, UND SCHWEIZERISCHE BANKGESELLSCHAFT

Werfthalle der Zürichsee-Schiffahrtsgesellschaft, Mythenquai 333, 8038 Zürich

Sa 15. August, 20 Uhr bis ca. 06.40 Uhr	Teile 1 - 3	
Di 18. August, 20 Uhr bis ca. 22.50 Uhr	Teil 1	
Mi 19. August, 20 Uhr bis ca. 22.50 Uhr	Teil 2	
Do 20. August, 20 Uhr bis ca. 23.30 Uhr	Teil 3	
Sa* 22. August, 20 Uhr bis ca. 06.40 Uhr	Teile 1 - 3	

Preise Teile 1 - 3 Samstag 15. und 22. August   Fr. 150.—/120.—
Preise Teil 1, 2 und 3 Di 18. bis Do 20. August Fr. 60.—/ 45.—
Keine Ermässigungen

Vorverkauf ab 3. Juli bei Jecklin (Tel. 251 59 00) und
Jelmoli (Tel. 211 97 97)

*Karten für diese Vorstellung sind ab 7. August ausschliesslich
im Vorverkauf des Zürcher Theater Spektakels erhältlich
(Billettzentrale Werdmühleplatz, Tel. 221 22 83)

Eine Veranstaltung der Präsidialabteilung der Stadt Zürich
im Rahmen von «India in Switzerland»
mit Unterstützung
der Schweizerischen Bankgesellschaft

Publikumsrestaurant mit indischen Spezialitäten an Vorstellungs-
tagen geöffnet ab 17 Uhr

In the multi-racial United States the internationalism of Brook's company was more on trial than anywhere else and it, not surprisingly, received more than a few knocks. Rising to anticipation of this, Brook gave his most eloquent and subtle interview during the whole of *The Mahabharata* life-span to a Los Angeles paper, explaining first the value of selecting performers from more than fifteen countries:

> Each actor has to have something that's different from the next. Contrast is the most ancient principle of any company. In the oldest *commedia dell'arte* and repertory companies you had a fat man, the saucy servant, the old man, the young lover. In our international group, we've never tried to do this on a United Nations basis, of, say, if we have two people from the East, we must have two from the West. But clearly, there is a strong mixture made by having a Japanese, an African, a Frenchman and an American playing together.

Brook insisted yet again that the use of an international troupe was not meant in any way to melt down the style into some kind of *esperanto* acting:

> You can't take a bit of Bali and a bit of Japan and a bit of Africa, and arrive at a synthesis. I believe in the opposite: fundamentally, all men are the same, and if only we were a little more developed, we would have within us what belongs to every culture. It's our misfortune that we are locked in little things called cultures. It doesn't interest me that our Japanese actor shows us the way they do it in Kabuki. What is interesting is that deep down he had evolved a certain individuality, which is searching to express the same human things as, but is different from, the individuality of the African. For us, it's the *same thing* that matters. In working together, the truth in *The Mahabharata* permeates until everyone sees that we're looking for the same thing, and then each one in telling it begins to call on his own natural vocabulary. If these vocabularies are serving the same essential purpose, they will fit together. In fact, you even come to a point where the African can make a Japanese movement, but that only arises through an osmosis, not through a synthesis.

If his interviewer began to feel he might be stalking what ultimately was inexpressible, Brook certainly stated more unequivocally than ever before what he thought was *The Mahabharata*'s main theme:

> It's about war, and conflict. More than any Greek tragedy that I

know, this vast story is like a prism looking from every direction at this mystery of human existence called conflict. One of the most powerful threads that goes through it is that it's a story told to a young man so that he can learn how to live through a most difficult, dangerous and terrible period of history – a period, like our own, of everything at an end-of-the-world explosion point.

How does a prism look from every direction? Brook may have been aware that it was a good sales pitch to make enormous claims for your product in Los Angeles – this was, after all, the home of some of the biggest publicity enterprises in the world.

The local critics responded predictably by calling *The Mahabharata* 'a trip like no other', 'pre-Christian soap opera', or saying, 'at times this group's symphony of accents can sound like a convention of New York cab drivers'. Another commentator praised the production as being 'wonderfully ecumenical to have the tale told in a variety of foreign accents'.

The even-handed *Los Angeles Herald Examiner* printed two reviews on the same page. In the first, Richard Stayton, the paper's theatre critic, found the lack of rapport between the Raleigh Studios' Stage 12 expansiveness and Brook's intimate style disturbing, contrasting *The Mahabharata* unfavourably with Ariane Mnouchkine's Théâtre du Soleil and her Shakespearian adaptations, which, even in French, camouflaged the impersonal studio atmosphere. It was, wrote Stayton, 'as if we're watching a biblical epic on screen . . . the company performed reverently, in an understated style, as if in a cathedral'. Stayton also found 'a lack of ensemble cohesion' and 'the sound and fury about two feuding factions of an ancient Hindu family begin to assume the melodramatic character of *Dynasty* or *Bonanza*'.

But in the second review Michael Lassell found Brook had 'changed his life' – for the second time, making him aware how 'narrow a wedge of the experiential pie we Westerners, especially Americans, have sliced off for ourselves'. The first revelation had happened some twenty years before:

I was a student in London struck dumb with grief by the Royal Shakespeare Company's 'U.S.', an indictment of the Vietnam War. Trembling with post-adolescent confusion, I wrote to the 'U.S.' company, demanding an answer: What should I do? There was no answer, just a note that my epistle had been read aloud to the company.

The company had been exhausted on their arrival in Los Angeles – as several reviewers were quick to point out – but in spite of the warm and spirited reception of large audiences it did not feel that the

West Coast really understood *The Mahabharata*. 'They laughed to show they were with it,' said Urs Bihler (Dushassana), 'but they wouldn't reach out to the spiritual thing.' The noise of people going in and out of the auditorium became disrupting during the marathons, and the acoustics, anyway, were bad. Audiences were issued with cushions and long lists of requirements to survive the night, and they had to be doing something all the time – eating, rustling, somehow showing they were there.

'Then came the time when the earth cracked,' recounted Bihler. There was danger of a second and more serious quake during the evening of a performance. Bihler was called upon to make an announcement during the interval. 'Here is a Swiss actor announcing their apocalypse. I made it in such a funny way to bring the house down.' He had to read from a small piece of paper:

> This building is new and exceeds seismic safety requirements.
> The seating is built in such a way that there is slight movement
> with normal usage. We have extra ushers in the audience today.
> Follow their instructions should a situation occur.

In October the production moved to the Majestic, New York, for a three month run: for an objective description of what Chloe Obolensky, the designer, had done to the interior of the theatre none surpassed that, again, of Michael Ratcliffe. (Great loyalty was shown by Brook's critic compatriots who followed *The Mahabharata* from country to country.)

> New York has gained a magnificent new performance space in
> the refurbished Majestic Theatre (1903) . . . An old vaudeville,
> legit and movie house, the Majestic has been gutted, modernised
> and decoratively 'distressed' by the painters to lay bare its
> chronology. Enlivening the grey here are patches of rose-madder
> and turquoise green (a very unusual combination in a theatre)
> and the back wall of the stage itself is a huge swathe of Pompeian
> red. The Bouffes du Nord is rather secretive and enclosing, like a
> baroque chapel or mosque, but the Majestic is populist and
> generous.

But while the majority of the middle-of-the-road New York critics respected *The Mahabharata*'s revamped home and themselves responded generously, the most influential names objected strongly. Frank Rich in the *New York Times* showed how little he was prepared to tolerate a stiff posterior in the cause of art:

To simulate the conditions of Mr Brook's working-class base of

Les Bouffes du Nord (and below)

operations in Paris, Les Bouffes du Nord, the theater has been artfully restored to a semi-dilapidated state, with chipped plaster, exposed brick, mottled paint and, for seating, punishingly hard benches. For this production, such chic, postmodern asceticism seems contrived – an environment for a Beverly Hills ashram rather than for a genuine rendition of a Hindu epic.

John Simon claimed that the 5 million dollars used for refurbishing the theatre 'like a gaudy artificial ruin' of the eighteenth century, was a prodigious waste of money. 'This publicly funded, expensive Temple of Dilapidation in an impoverished neighbourhood that could have used the money better will be there after Brook majestically returns to Paris; who and what can be fitted into it then?'

More fair in his judgment, and maintaining reservations about the 'distastefully fake . . . genteel shabbiness in a beggary-chic haute couture style', Clive Barnes found the main part of the renovation terrific:

> It uses the existing proscenium arch (which remained structurally undamaged after all the building's vicissitudes) but provides a huge new thrust stage. The new seating capacity is only 905 but the relationship between stage and audience has a marvellous immediacy.

Similarly sour in their response to the play and the acting, Frank Rich and John Simon did their best to turn the New York run into a disaster. Simon peddled cheap cracks – 'What is not in *The Mahabharata*, says the text of the poem, is not to be found anywhere else in the world, which, on reflection, is a good thing, or life would be even longer and drearier' – and he pretentiously attacked its wordiness: 'hours of logorrheic theater – great philosophic-poetic palaver, worthy of Gurdjieff or Kahlil Gibran, Carlos Castaneda or Shirley MacLaine'. He ended his review with a personal insult: 'In the *Times*, Frank Rich styled Brook "one of the great theater minds of our time"; too bad it is cracked.'

Frank Rich's strictures were more considered, and therefore more serious: Brook's script was 'mostly prosaic, sometimes unidiomatic English'. It became spoken by an international company whose English was, in many cases 'an awkward second language'. Carrière's ingenious 'dare-devil screenplay-writing stunt' covered too much ground and was therefore 'by necessity more often recited than dramatised'. Some of the acting, for example Bruce Myers' Krishna, which Rich called 'a Ralph Richardson role if ever there was one', was showy and over-vocalised. Finally the whole work appeared 'less a distillation of its source than a busy condensation'.

The snobby, condescending *New Yorker* reviewer pushed some of Rich's points into absurdity, calling the whole production 'spiritual terrorism' – 'the kind of theater created by a lot of people hitting things, rolling about on the floor and pouring things on themselves. There are engaging moments and even one or two jokes'. The *New Yorker* also attacked Brook personally: 'It's a shame that Peter Brook was less interested in metaphor than in editorializing. For metaphors are really his field.'

Many of the actors found themselves devastated and demoralised by these reviews, although by far the majority were full of praise and appreciation. And, reviews apart, the actors felt themselves under great pressure in New York. Andrzej Seweryn declared that 'The New York theatre world was not interested. I had waited for some deep welcome. I didn't have a real meeting.' Three or four others became ill or not able to play; Ryszard Cieslak lost his voice. One night Vittorio Mezzogiorno completely lost confidence and shouted an obscenity in the middle of a speech. Everyone had to work twice as hard to establish the production, although Brook reassured them, 'If we were on Broadway now we would just stop, but we are lucky because seventy-five or eighty per cent of the tickets are sold out. This could be an advantage, for now we will have an audience which will be really interested'.

Involved as Brook was in rehearsing *The Cherry Orchard* for its New York opening, he refused to become embroiled in the actors' struggles and insecurities, simply telling them that the time to discuss the problems was not right. There was a crisis, too, about the future of the tour and the finance for the film.

The cast, left to itself to sink or swim, struggled hard and courageously. 'I had a lot of time to look in the audience,' reported Bihler, 'they were very blasé.' Not everybody felt the same way. Lloyd claimed, 'We had wonderful audiences. It's ridiculous to say, when you've been written off by two critics, "We were rejected by New York".' Mamadou Dioume (Bhima) loved New York, and felt completely at home there. So did Antonin Stahly-Vishwanadan (the boy), who, when Nolan Hemmings injured a ligament, took over the role of Abhimanyu.

The final figures for the New York run vindicated Brook: ninety-seven per cent of all seats had been sold, while gross receipts exceeded $1.5 million. 'I adored it,' Clive Barnes delivered his judgment well after the first night, 'with a clear mind and a bum not noticeably numbed.' William Wilkinson, as producer of the tour, claimed that the production had matured, 'had gained security, confidence, energy.'

In Australia, for the first time with the English version, they emerged into the open air. It opened in Perth on 2 February 1988, in the disused Boya granite quarry in Mundaring, three-quarters of an hour's drive from the centre of Western Australia's capital. 'Take mozzie annihilants. And take a warm hat. It was 40°C in Perth last Saturday afternoon. Twelve hours later a cold easterly wind had blown up fit to snap-freeze the ears and pierce the forehead,' advised one columnist; 'Take a piss before each part,' said the tour manager, Mark Gould.

The effect was spectacular. Barry Oakley travelled from Sydney to see it:

> Pilgrims, we rest here and eat and use the portable lavatories (from vindaloo to Portaloo).
>
> A man in a white garment, looking like Moses, summons us with the Indian equivalent of a ram's horn. We file around a rocky outcrop, climb flight after flight of shaky steps, take our seats in the temporary stand, and look down.
>
> It's a wonderful sight; a twilit cliff of granite, interlocking planes of black and brown, like an enormous Fred Williams painting. And below, on the quarry floor, a gleaming performance area of sand and water.
>
> At the side, overtopped by a pile of massive stones, stands Peter Brook, stocky and confident. Where have I seen that look of paternal benevolence before? On the faces of evangelists, as they prepare to impart their message.

While Oakley found the script needed 'a vulgar untranscendental script-editor', he surrendered completely to the magic of the spectacle, 'An unforgettable epilogue gives us an image of paradise'.

Hyperbole was common. Brian Hoad wrote in *The Bulletin*:

> So it was, on a starry summer's night in a sandy arena crossed by a stream beneath the towering cliffs of the quarry surrounded by the timeless bush and wafted by winds from the Indian Ocean, Brook and his 30 actors and musicians of every race and color opened their hearts in friendship and enveloped their audience in a fabulous spiritual journey: magic fires spurted from the earth, spirits were evoked, voices warned from heaven; great drums throbbed, conch shells groaned, flutes wailed; the pomp of kings was summoned up in great swirls of red silk, magicians levitated and fierce battles raged . . .

At the end, reported Lance Campbell in the *Perth Advertiser*, the sun was at the rim of the world: 'The shadows are back. War is almost over. "The sun is slowly rising on 18 million corpses," says Vyasa, not to mention the 900 still breathing, who proved it by laughing.'

Teacher Dale Irving found this time the most disturbing and the most rewarding. 'To have the battle scenes so early in the morning was weird and quite upsetting,' she said, 'then with the dawn came the final resolution. It was a monumental feeling, utterly unique.'

The cast of *The Mahabharata* found that while the Perth quarry was dark and difficult, with nature – in the form of the bitter winds and even, sometimes, falling rocks – menacing art ('Peter loves to direct storms,' said one actress), in Adelaide the calcium chalk, Greek white rocks were 'full of light'. The district of Anstey Hill in Southern Australia was more civilised, with indications of a deep Germanic influence. The preparations at the quarry itself were elaborate; $142,000 (£70,000) had been spent in building a cement bordered river and pond, with boulders to conceal the lighting and scaffolding towers. The quarry face and its surroundings had been adapted and improved, and a 'theatrical village' provided to maintain the actors and their costumes. This quarry had first been used in 1980 as a theatre for *Conference of the Birds*.

With audiences of VIPs, *The Mahabharata* would become the 'in' theatrical event, predicted one commentator. Perth deserved a pat on the back, wrote Anna-Maria Dell'Oso, because:

> glamorous opening nights with limousines, red carpets, champagne and the rustle of designer silk are not its style. Perhaps because the Sydney–Melbourne white-wine arts mafia and the radical Swinburne-AFTS (angry young penguins) find it too far to drive or hitchhike, the bars and foyers are refreshingly free of Balmain-Parkville gossip or Film News feminist-semiotic anguish.

The seating reached a 'Grand Prix gold standard', and seats for marathon performances, which were quickly sold out, cost $118. The quarry held 1,247 people and some criticism was levelled at the food and facilities: during performances the queues for loos swelled to such enormity that some people headed up the slopes in desperation. Australians drolly noted this kind of detail: 'Again the interval was inadequate. There were complaints that the Indian food had run out and fears, from some of those who had eaten, about the possibly embarrassing repercussions of having eaten dhal.'

'I know actors have to suffer for their art, but do they have to take us along, too?' demanded one querulous patron. Some of the audience found the spiritual experience overrated – a reaction more commonly registered in Australia than elsewhere. Another spectator reacted, 'I think Mr Brook is having us all on'; several critics regretted the omission of any catharsis, or the delivery of a great moral blow: 'a fine piece of high culture but not great art. There's just too much blood on the sand.'

'Quite symbolically the play begins at sunset and culminates at sunrise,' wrote William Burdett-Coutts, who jumboed all the way from Glasgow. He found the sun setting 'across an earth-burnt valley of vineyards: a deep red orison that sat heavy and gloatingly above the horizon, seemingly mocking the pilgrims fighting their way to seats.' Burdett-Coutts' pen registered the best intervention of nature in these outdoor performances:

> Amusingly there was one moment when an actress exclaimed, 'I go', and at that very moment a gust of wind wrapped a reed mat around her, holding her still. Nature and artifice met in a deft, unexpected action, but one which seemed to carry a significance to the whole production.

Bob Lloyd lived by himself in the quarry, staying in one of the dressing-caravans, and between the performances wandered about in what he called a 'beautiful bit of land beyond the quarry'. It became home, and the administration had installed a children's swimming-pool where he could bathe, and enjoy the sun. 'I could play at being a primitive,' he said, 'and I had a car for going to the supermarket. I had fifteen acres of varied land at my disposal, a planet in miniature with no-one in it.' For him nature and illusion intermingled. Vyasa starts the play by building a fire and before each performance Lloyd would gather twigs, enjoying the 'weld between real life and theatrical spectacle'.

So ended the 'great all-night Aussie picnic'.

The streets outside the old gasworks in Copenhagen were coated in late spring snow when *The Mahabharata* descended into Europe for the second time. 'It's larger than all of us,' said Ciaran Hinds, the Irish actor, who played Nakula and Aswatthaman, 'it has a special life force.' But one may perhaps question what its force would have amounted to without the hyper-sophisticated fleets of 747s.

There were cast changes in Copenhagen, particularly among the women, because Mallika Sarabhai left temporarily to make a film and Miriam Goldschmidt played Draupadi. Here they enacted the marathon during the daytime: all the cast were agreed these marathon performances were very special. But the culmination of the whole tour arrived on 13 April, 1988, when *The Mahabharata* entered its Glaswegian limelight. Everything, unconsciously, in the majority of the company, had been building up to this moment.

Glasgow's dynamic initiative and once again Chloe Obolensky's inspired transformation of the Old Transport Museum, a former tram-shed – 'We don't have sets so the set is the building itself,' the technical director Jean-Guy Lecat informed the awe-struck Glaswegians – induced considerable soul-searching and recrimination in the London papers. 'One in the eye for Edinburgh and a timely cosmopolitan blow in the goolies for London,' wrote Michael

Coveney in the London *Financial Times*. All tickets for the six all-night marathon performances had been sold out two months ahead of opening, but there were five other three night cycles, scheduled for the expansive, but intimate, Victorian Palace which combined the best aspects of out-of-doors performance with those of the enclosed space.

Brook at the Glasgow press conference *(Photograph by Alan Wylie)*

'England was the ultimate proving place,' pronounced Vittorio Mezzogiorno not quite picking up the nationalistic nuances of the place name Glasgow. His thought was echoed by everyone else in the cast. They were now ready to give the best performances of the tour, knowing that, for the marathons, at least, they would be playing to audiences of their discriminating and theatrical peers, shuttle-loaded *cognoscenti* from London and the South-East, keen to witness what the British press now generally hailed as 'the theatrical event of the decade'.

The production rose to its audiences' highest expectations. 'Suddenly in Glasgow it acquired relaxation,' said William Wilkinson. 'They relaxed into it so they played with every little effect clear – they knew just where to pitch it, and hold it. I was immensely proud.'

The press achieved a degree of unanimity, style and authority which made a few of the Australian and particularly some of the American responses seem, by comparison, uncouth and ill-informed.

Overnight *The Mahabharata*, from satisfying the international culture-vulture circuit, became elevated into high art. Michael Ratcliffe, who had seen it just about everywhere, yet again vividly recreated the impact for his *Observer* readers:

> The space is simple: a three-sided seat-stand faces an open stage contained by new brick wings at the sides – the pointing glopped on like ice-cream – and a reasonably undistressed terracotta wall at the back . . . The little pool at the front of the stage and the shallow, bridged stream across the back are in place as before, while the clothes and special effects have never looked better. The simplicity provides a perfect setting for the explosion of colour, elegance and superb tailoring unleashed by Chloe Obolensky's Indian costumes – orange, saffron, scarlet, magenta, mulberry, cobalt-blue and ink-black.
>
> The use of fire remains exceptional. No one who sees it will ever forget the vision of the great archer Arjuna, conjured in the forest by his enemies behind a three-foot wall of flame. The thin cloud of dazzling white smoke that drifts like poison gas above the heads of the prostrate warriors and into the audience is scarcely less extraordinary.

Bernard Levin in *The Times* commented on the spiritual message:

> But the great undying stories from the innocent ancient world will live forever, and the reason can be seen in Glasgow at this very moment. It is because, for all the lurid stories, the impossible bargains and inexorable tragedies, the mysterious figures and their mysterious intentions, the unresolved conflicts and the insoluble puzzles, they are as meaningful and important to us today as ever they were to their audiences and readers over the millennia.

Practically every critic picked up the Shakespearean resonance and concentration that Brook had been attempting to achieve: for instance, Michael Coveney found that Ryszard Cieslak as Dhritharashtra invoked 'Lear and that play's persistent imagery of seeing through blindness. He demands information, searching his personal darkness with a jaw-jutting, watery-eyed blow-torch intensity.' When Mireille Maalouf (Gandhari) said, 'Give me my veil,' she intoned the words like 'a forbear of Cleopatra'.

The battle scenes were constantly placed on a par with those of Shrewsbury and Bosworth. Eric Shorter in the *Daily Telegraph* compared the whole effect to Peter Hall's treatment of the Wars of the Roses in the 1960s, in which he found the action resembled that of the second and third part. (Brook had been in Stratford during that crucial season.) Catherine Lockerbie related in *The Scotsman* how Shakespearean themes forcefully struck the mind – 'the tormented bastard (Karna) pitting his bitter strength against the world, ghostly, bloodied figures relating slaughter, the power of filial love and brotherly hatred'. While the eminent Shakespearean director, John Barton, co-director with Hall and adaptor of the Wars of the Roses, told Michael Birkett, 'That's the greatest production we'll ever see.'

Only John Peter, in the *Sunday Times*, carefully qualified his approval of Brook's brilliantly inventive production. The 'huge applause' at the end had an ingredient of complicity – for ever since Wagner the 'marathon art event has bred an audience of ecstatic self-discipline'. Peter found the 'density of the story' not equal to its playing time, while 'some of its actors were almost incomprehensible'. It was time, he concluded, 'for Brook to return to an ordinary theatre, preferably in Britain'.

If *The Mahabharata* had almost revelled in earthy surroundings and popular acclaim in Glasgow – appealing like a Shakespearean mechanical to Scot and English groundlings, then at the Ginza Saison Theatre in Tokyo, for the final stage of its tour, it once again entered the category of 'high cultural event'.

Some of the Japanese press comments appeared like specific replies to John Peter. 'A powerful social comment as to how civilisations can work together,' wrote Makoto Oooka in *Asahi Newspaper*: while Hitomi Nakamura in the *Japan Times Weekly*

described how 'The various foreign accents of the players create a wonderful atmosphere on stage.' Takashi Nomura found that as

> *The Mahabharata* is a portrait of all human races past, present and future, as well as the universal destiny; and in this sense, I understood this piece of work as something surpassing Wagner's *Ring* . . . a magnificent creation of mythology . . . an immense and divine work only possible for Mr Brook.

The reverential silence with which the Japanese audiences followed the action puzzled, and even unnerved, the players in the fourteenth-floor sky-scraper theatre. Corraface commented that, with all the futurist metallic girders around, it was like being part of a video game. 'It was strange,' said Mezzogiorno, 'they were absolutely silent; didn't move or laugh . . . But they brought us flowers, they were touched.' This was explained by Maalouf: 'The public still treats the theatre as a sacred place'; her husband Seweryn regretted the little social contact they could make with Japanese actors.

Everywhere they went people greeted them as if they themselves were the characters of *The Mahabharata*: 'In Japan I didn't feel it was my country,' commented Yoshi Oida (Drona) uneasily; Jeffrey Kissoon (Karna) echoed his sentiment – 'I didn't like Tokyo.'

Bihler believed that the Japanese, for all their enthusiastic reaction, just could not work out the meaning of the first part, 'The Game of Dice', but as soon as the story advanced into fighting and death, it 'changes into something else' with which they could identify completely. As for Bob Lloyd, a chain-smoker, he planned to stop smoking before the last marathon in Tokyo – 'I sort of prayed for the first time in my life' – and he succeeded.

The final word on the Japanese reaction should be given to Takashi Nomura:

> The troupe of actors are from 18 countries, and Director, Mr Peter Brook reformed (sic) this time Japan performance into further desirable shape.
>
> Since *MAHABHARATA* requires audience extraordinary time-sequence (more than 8 hours), we audience can't help but expecting a huge amount of exhaustion. However, the reality was on the contrary. We could obtain very comfortable satisfaction and fulfilment.
>
> The success was proved in the way of standing applause and many times of curtain call from the audience who never tried to leave the seats until the end, which has been quite unusual here in Japan.

4

Vehicles for gods

God expects but one thing of you, and that is that you should come out of yourself in so far as you are a created being and let God be in you.
ECKHART

Brook has written that in Haitian voodoo all you need for a ceremony is a pole and some people. The people beat drums, chant and drink, while far away in Africa the gods hear the call. The pole links the visible and invisible worlds, for when the gods fly in some six or seven hours later, they cross through it into one of the crowd – they must have a human vehicle. The one chosen gives a kick, a moan or two, or thrashes about on the ground. No longer himself, he has become possessed. And the god now has a form. The ordinary man or woman, according to Brook, 'can talk to him, pump his hand, argue, curse him, go to bed with him – and so, nightly, the Haitian is in contact with the great powers and mysteries that rule his day'.

For *The Mahabharata* Brook himself had to circle the world many times to bring the demi-gods and superhuman beings out of India and into the souls of his actors. With Carrière he had inaugurated an original approach to casting: using Carrière's script, with the playwright in attendance, Brook auditioned actors from all parts of the world. Brook then made Carrière, in front of the actors, play the characters. From then on possession became a complicated, sometimes miraculous, process. Some actors, when the work came to be filmed, believed that only then had they become fully changed into the personages they were conveying. Some, with the crude practicality of Haitian voodoo, had been penetrated straight away. Others resisted in differing degrees. Several switched from one character to playing another.

They were, and remained, strong individuals. 'You can never have a group with strong individuals,' said Jeffrey Kissoon, an Indian born in Trinidad, who studied drama at a teacher training college in Warwick, England. He acted Karna, implacable foe of the Pandavas, although, unknown to himself, their elder brother. Kissoon added, 'But there are no stars – we are all stars.'

Each of these individuals, highly recognisable as 'Brooktian' actors, had a definite nationality, yet their nationality did not impose on their character. For example, Yoshi Oida played Drona, the

Jeffrey Kissoon

Brahmin sage and master of arms, like a Japanese and not like a Japanese. He brought to Drona the essential sympathy and heroism from his own culture that he recognised in Drona, yet he also made the character into a unique and timeless individual. His 'supranationalism' was the product of working with Brook for twenty years.

If *The Mahabharata* is the universal story of mankind – 'the mirror in which every human being can see him or herself', as Oida called it – the actor himself, as Hamlet says, also holds a mirror up to nature. Brook's actors employed their own national characteristics, but were endowed with something extra – an essence of universality, an appeal which crossed boundaries. Brook's method of work drew from each a range of expression that not only freed him or her to receive the character, but made the meaning as broad as it could conceivably be.

How do you achieve the magic and directness of a children's folk-tale, of scripture, and of myth and legend everywhere? The Italian Vittorio Mezzogiorno confronted with the problem of playing the legendary warrior Arjuna, son of Indra, king of the gods, related that the words of Brook that helped the most – and, typically, were said to someone else and only overheard – were 'To think of playing a god is madness'.

Brook never generalised. In fact *The Mahabharata* achieved its universality by being, at every point, clear and specific. Paradoxically – and completely unlike modern attempts to collectivise religious texts and universalise rituals – its richness was one of a deepened and concentrated image. Taking the best from each country he distilled it, or painted it deeper and harder, so it stood out. As Kissoon pointed out, 'Peter's intention is to simplify': Mamadou Dioume, who played the giant, demi-god Bhima, called it 'imagination instead of determination'.

The distinctive and gaunt six-foot-five frame, and finely sculpted head, of Sotigui Kouyate as the ideal celibate warrior-god, Bhisma, had a powerful and unforgettable presence both on stage and on screen. In the latter in particular, in close-up, Kouyate's radiant spiritual quality underlined Bhisma's renunciation: 'To avoid all conflict, and for love of my father, I swear the oath of absolute renunciation. I will say it clearly, I abjure forever the love of woman.'

Kouyate, a fifty-three year old 'Griot' from Upper Volta, is a highly sophisticated and all-round actor, dancer, singer and composer who has appeared in many African, German and French films. 'Can I play God?' he asked me when I met him at Joinville studio. 'No, it's stupid; you have to be yourself plus "something", a force which is beyond you.'

Kouyate with Carole Fèvre

He had first created the role of Bhisma in the French version. I was struck by his relaxed Parisian manner and beautifully cut suit of black and grey silk, with leather-trimmed collar and pockets: not at all that of a sombre acolyte of high art. Yet he had, naturally, a stillness and timeless broad appeal, which might easily and instinctively have adjusted themselves to absorbing the presence of a god.

He found it very difficult. Bhisma is the son of a goddess. Although he finally takes up arms on the side of the Kauravas, his sympathies lie with the Pandavas because he knows they have no father on earth, and they were stripped bare of their lands and cheated of their possessions in the game of dice.

It had been, in Kouyate's case, the twelve-day trip he and the cast made as part of their preparatory work on *The Mahabharata* – in particular the effect of the omnipresence of Hinduism – which helped him to understand the problem. The 'profound attachment of the people to their religion and how it was truly part of their life', gave him the solution. 'I had, *at the same time,* to be both man and god: never something in between the two.'

'Krishna is you and me, and fire and water.' The English actor, Bruce Myers, who had been with Brook from the mid-1960s, asked the same question as Kouyate, yet in a different way. Krishna, incarnation of the god Vishnu, descends on earth with his supernatural power to save *dharma,* to restore the equilibrium which is menaced by the conflict of the Pandavas and the Kauravas. He has to accept his role, namely that while as a god he can order destiny, as a man all he can do is to try to prevent the war, while still knowing it is inevitable. Krishna, therefore, is a highly ambiguous figure – 'he does not answer questions' – and he even dies like a human. That 'there is no certain way', according to Myers, sums him up.

'The key to being Krishna,' Myers finally resolved, was that 'if you know something is going to happen, you are calm.' Parallel to the playing of Krishna, who sees people piercingly, who is unscrupulous and resorts to tricks and lies to save the principle of harmony in the world, Myers observed that the more he worked with Brook, 'the more I see what can be achieved through calmness than through dynamism'.

Myers became completely fused with his role and deeply enjoyed Krishna's compassionate observation of the world – his fascination with 'people avoiding what they are, and being what they are'. Krishna is 'lightness' – but a lightness which comes by passing through many stages. Myers believed Brook himself identified strongly with Krishna's enlightenment, and liked the idea of a reality of non-being beyond the world's illusion: an ambiguity central to all of life.

'You might then ask where the emotion is in Krishna?' Myers

claimed that Brook's answer to this would be that it is 'not personal'. This was echoed by the diminutive Algerian Jewish actor, Maurice Benichou, the French Krishna, whom French critics credited with a smile more mysterious than the Mona Lisa. 'You must not act Krishna, but be present,' said Benichou.

What drew Mireille Maalouf to *The Mahabharata,* although she had worked frequently with Brook since 1975, was the theme of war. Born in Paris, of Christian Lebanese and French parentage, she grew up in Beirut where she studied law. With dark, classical features and a compelling beauty, Maalouf played two key roles in both the French and English stage productions: Ganga, goddess of the sacred river, the Ganges – the mother of Bhisma – and the Princess Gandhari, who, on marrying the blind king, Dhritharashtra, binds up her eyes and embraces voluntary blindness. It is Gandhari who gives birth to a hundred sons, the Kauravas.

Maalouf strongly identified the war between the Pandavas and Kauravas – not only a civil war, but a family war in which every warrior on both sides is somehow related – with what has continued without end in the Lebanon. For her, Gandhari is a complete, far-seeing woman. She binds her eyes to live in equality with her husband: a great act of love on which she never goes back. People have reproached Gandhari for her submissiveness, but Maalouf dismissed this, emphasising that she is both human and tough – the only one who takes Krishna to task for the underhand and scheming way he runs the war. 'It's the same thing in the Lebanon, I can cry out against it, but nothing changes.'

Mireille Maalouf

The small part of Ganga (omitted from the film version) was her favourite of the two roles: Ganga is the river goddess who appears as a woman of a beauty that beggars description, who lives with her husband Santanu in boundless love, but who every year wraps her new-born child in a piece of cloth and throws him in the river. As she has already dictated to Santanu that he will never challenge or oppose her actions, be neither curious nor angry, nor ask any questions 'on pain of seeing me leave you instantly', he stays quiet until the eighth year when he cannot restrain himself any more, and asks why she is killing all her children. She answers him that as Ganga, goddess of the river, she is not killing her babies but setting them free by returning them to their divine origin. But the eighth, Bhisma, she says, will live – 'infallible, invincible' – then she vanishes with the child, returning only twenty years later to present the fully grown young man to his father.

As Ganga, Maalouf had to suggest that she carried a torrent and was, simultaneously, both a goddess and a very feminine and attractive woman passing through a number of stages quickly – almost an abstraction of a role. She described this transparency of non-being as needing incredibly precise and exact preparation, even to the extent of making sure, nightly, the creases in her veil were correctly ironed and fell in exactly the same place. She had to act 'without formulating gestures' and signify something concrete and true without making it smaller – add another *'colorato'* she called it, a 'special note or dimension'. Hard although it was for her to put her finger on it exactly – how can one describe possession, when one is simply possessed? – she felt just as passionately involved after four years of playing this one page of text as she had been on the first night.

Andrzej Seweryn, blond-haired, heroic looking, who enhanced with mysterious, Christ-like power the role of the Pandava Yudhishthira – son of Kunti and of Dharma, the god of earthly harmony – played his diametric opposite Duryodhana in the French version. Ferocious and evil and first-born of the Kauravas, Duryodhana desires rulership of the whole earth. These two characters, more than any of the others, hold *The Mahabharata* on its course of action.

'I accept not to understand,' Seweryn declared. 'I try not to pretend to be more intelligent than these extraordinary characters – it's like me saying I am more intelligent than Hamlet, which would be stupid.' Born in East Germany, Seweryn grew up in his parents' native Poland. He made numerous films – winning major awards for leading roles in two Andrzej Wajda pictures – and acted classical roles such as Ruy Blas and Don Carlos on the stage: a romantic actor of tremendous power, a sort of Polish equivalent of Gérard Philipe.

Seweryn saw Duryodhana as an idealist who, at one moment,

Seweryn with Chloe Obolensky

succumbed to a terrible weakness: not a conventionally evil character but, as his father, Dhritharashtra, describes him – 'He's blind and he attracts disaster.' 'In India,' said Seweryn, 'we learnt that in Sanskrit the same kind of good – evil dualism does not exist.' Duryodhana, bent on achieving power and keeping it, is the nearest in the play to a godless egotist: 'He has no need of the gods, nor of heaven, which is why he has to be exterminated.' Born a hundredth part, like each of his brothers, of the stone ball that issued from Gandhari, he can command mightier forces than the five sons of the gods he is bent on destroying.

But at the end, paradoxically, detested as he is, his legs smashed in a cheap trick played on him by Bhima, Duryodhana witnesses the terrible destruction wrought by Aswatthaman on the Pandava camp and dies happily. 'I reigned on earth, I was just. I laughed, I sang, I loved my friends and my wives . . . I knew all human joys. Conflict is a necessary part of man's emotional dualism: we cannot judge, but we must accept the consequences.'

The notion is profoundly Hindu: condemned by destiny to what he is, Duryodhana achieves his *dharma*. Blindness had been passed on to him in a mental form from his father, and, right to the end, he carries no regret of individual responsibility for his wickedness. Duryodhana reaches Paradise: 'He has,' said Seweryn, 'realised his *dharma.*'

Seweryn found Yudhishthira, his role in the English and film versions, much easier to identify with. Although all the characters harbour qualities which oppose their central nature, Yudhishthira, for all the shadows he harbours in his personality, approaches an occidental hero more closely than any other character.

We see much of the story through his eyes, while we turn to him, instinctively, to see how he will react to the latest shock of an unforeseen event. But, like Dostoevsky's Prince Mishkin, Yudhishthira is also a holy fool: 'He is the only one who hesitates.' As the intellectual Pandava who nimbly answers the riddles by the lake where his brothers have drunk and become poisoned, Yudhishthira proves to the voice of the lake, who is Dharma in disguise, that inside him there reposes enough universal wisdom to win back his brothers their life. This is his catechism.

> What is quicker than the wind? *Thought.** What can cover the earth? *Darkness.* Who are the more numerous, the living or the dead? *The living, because the dead are no longer.* Give me an example of space. *My two hands as one.* An example of grief. *Ignorance.* Of poison. *Desire.* An example of defeat. *Victory.* What is the cause of the world. *Love.* What is your opposite? *Myself.* What is madness? *A forgotten way.* Why do men revolt? *To find beauty, either in life or in death.* What for each of us is inevitable? *Happiness.* And what is the greatest marvel? *Each day, death strikes and we live as though we were immortal. This is what is the greatest marvel.*
>
> * (Y.'s answers are given in italics).

But Yudhishthira's tastes for gambling and perfection also precipitate the war that leaves eighteen million slain on the battlefield. 'There is no answer,' commented Seweryn, 'to why Yudhishthira does not stop playing dice before he has lost his possessions, his land, his brothers, and finally his – and their – wife Draupadi.' It seems an extreme *dharma* to have to realise, but, even so, Seweryn found that he drew upon his own Christianity, especially in the commandment 'Thou shalt not kill'. While he understood the openness of Hinduism, and its acceptance of evil, *The Mahabharata* did not convert him to Brook's belief in the 'essential degeneracy' of Western Christianity: 'No one has proved to me that the love Christ has proposed to us is not a unique thing to follow and respect'. Seweryn married Mireille Maalouf in New York Town Hall during *The Mahabharata*'s visit to New York; Brook was their witness.

During the filming of *The Mahabharata* Mireille was expecting a baby, so, unlike her stage characters who between them give birth to a hundred and eight babies, she had, for reasons dictated by film-insurance underwriters, to withdraw from the cast. When, earlier, she was thinking of having a baby, and was not yet pregnant, she asked Brook, 'What do you think about the question of the baby or the film?' Brook, who gave her the go-ahead (in no way anticipating the absurd and later objection) told her, 'I would never hesitate. When you leave this life you don't take films or houses with you.'

Hélène Patarot as Gandhari

For saying this to her Mireille judged Brook: 'Before being an artist he is a unique human being with something which is disappearing from this world – a *sens de valeur.*'

'I must forget the light,' pointed out Ryszard Cieslak, also Polish, cast as the old blind king, Dhritharashtra. Cieslak worked with the Polish director Jerzy Grotowski for twenty-five years. As an expert in 'self-penetration', which Grotowski taught him, and 'in engaging in a sort of psychic conflict with the audience', Cieslak felt more prepared, perhaps, than some of the others for the assumption of a mythical character of Indian legend. His first impression, for instance, of Glenda Jackson, some twenty years before in *U.S.*, had been that she was 'like a mouse in the corner' – hardly the first idea that comes to mind about Glenda Jackson.

Cieslak observed that the blind fell into two categories, those born blind and those not born blind, who could therefore use their muscles. He tried to react through his muscles; but primarily, to portray the blindness, he looked inside himself and so to a large extent playing Dhritharashtra became an 'autobiographical' process. His blue-green watery eyes, anyway, were 'incredible sensitive', he told me in his broken English, and he went as far as showing, in Dhritharashtra's blindness, that colours in clothes could make a blind person's eyes move.

Cieslak's part exemplifies more than any other in *The Mahabharata* the struggle from the darkness of ignorance to the illumination of understanding. Gandhari's veil is taken off, on his command, when both of them reach Paradise, 'the last illusion'. He regains his sight. 'There was a time,' said Cieslak, 'when I was against *Mahabharata*. For as an actor I am almost naked – my soul in me inside. I have to show myself.' So he held back for a long time from joining the company, kept Brook waiting for four months, until he discovered the contemporary relevance of the work and it became a 'big pleasure to show the audience that it was like today'.

In Hinduism woman occupies a very different role from the one idealised in Christianity. Mallika Sarabhai, who played Draupadi, the woman married to the five demi-god Pandavas, complained that at first this ideal creature whom she had worshipped since childhood had been awfully misrepresented in the Brook–Carrière version. In Carrière's early scripts Draupadi 'had been portrayed as a wimp'. Both men were 'white' and did not understand 'the violence of an Indian woman and how, historically, women have never been secondary to men'. Particularly of significance, she found, was the omission of *shakti,* the female principle without which the world does not function. She questioned why Draupadi had so little to do, why many of her scenes had been omitted, in favour of the dramatised 'masculine warrior side'. Brook and Carrière would not at first let her utter the curses on the Kauravas, nor wash her hair in blood: 'Sometimes they were open and sometimes they were not.' She argued her case passionately.

There were heated differences during rehearsals. 'You know,' Brook told her one day, 'working with you is like working with Princess Margaret.' 'I said, "Why, have you ever worked with Princess Margaret?" ' 'Don't stand there like a dancer,' he reproved her at another time when they clashed. 'When Peter gets angry he goes very red in the face and very silent. He goes redder and redder as if he would burst.' She resisted his will, but had the 'strong feeling that someone has to be broken down and recreated'.

Just before opening in Avignon, she related, Brook gave way to her demands and allowed Draupadi her full stature. In the preparation work she would have liked to see more of *ananda*, which is Sanskrit for bliss at the deepest level – the bliss of creation – but she still felt at the end, after some hard tussles and differences of opinion, that Brook had made her a better actress. 'He taught me to peel away my character like an onion and find the nothing that is there at the centre.' She and Brook together were what another actor in *The Mahabharata* called 'the rubbing together of two sticks to make a spark', while Brook's assistant pointed out *'cette friction aide'*.

Sarabhai also viewed Draupadi as an ideal of contemporary woman: her five husbands never question her actions, while she is the only one in the marriage to argue – a reflection both on her intellectual qualities, and on their understanding. Above all, during all the conflict, she holds firm and, when her husbands want to give up fighting, she pushes them on, knowing there will be no result other than grief.

Sarabhai was staggered, while they were playing *The Mahabharata* in Perth, when, at a 'meet-the-artist' conference, a spiky-haired young woman denounced the play as patriarchal, sexist literature. Her impassioned rebuttal of this brought wild cheers from the audience. 'One Indian person, a woman, at the centre, is of great value,' Brook had pronounced. As the sole Indian in the cast she delivered her final judgment. 'I am proud as an Indian to be in the play. Had I not thought it was a proper representation of *The Mahabharata*, the product of a loving and true attitude, I would not have taken part.'

Erika Alexander joined the cast in New York and did not know who Peter Brook was before late 1987. In Los Angeles the parts of Madri and Hidimbi, the demoness, had been played by Tamsir Niane from Senegal, but she left the cast in order to marry and so a local actress had to be found, at all possible speed, to replace her. Erika, aged seventeen, was in her third week at New York University studying Arts and Humanities, but she had an agent and had already worked in the theatre. She was flown out to Los Angeles to meet Brook and to view the show. 'From the first moment I saw it I thought it the most beautiful thing I'd seen in my life . . . I never once hated this play.' She joined in enthusiastically with everything, especially the improvisations – 'Brook is so big on improvisations that something good must happen' – and she found her director completely dependable. 'I always had a problem of my voice going very high when I get excited. Peter says, "Don't squeak".'

What would happen after *The Mahabharata* was over? 'I don't know; will there be a life after *The Mahabharata*? I will go back to

New York. It will probably be the biggest thing that happens to me.'

'The passage of strong feelings through someone engaged in strong physical activity is very healthy . . . But there is a price. The material you use to create these imaginary people is your flesh and blood.' Yoshi Oida (Drona), who was nearing the age of sixty in fact looked a good ten years younger. He first joined Brook for Barrault's ill-fated experimental season of 1968, and has been with Brook since the Centre began. He is a small man, slight of build, with cropped, silvery hair. He trained under Okura, a Noh theatre master, but never acted in Noh theatre. He believed Brook chooses actors who have an affinity with himself.

'He won't use actors who stick in their past – you have to look for possibilities of change. With fear, with fame, with pride people don't open to the public. I could work with Peter. He doesn't like extravagance. He uses the minimum thing for maximum effect. He leaves space for your own imagination.'

Like Yoshi Oida, Vittorio Mezzogiorno was famous in his own country as a film star before he joined Brook. Mezzogiorno is a Neapolitan who learned English especially for the role of Arjuna. When he originally rehearsed with Brook for the French version of *The Mahabharata,* he had, to begin with, no key to understanding the character. He complained that as the central warrior-god, Arjuna had no psychology: 'Perfect, beautiful, strong, good, without problems . . .' Confronted with these demands he completely lost confidence in himself.

In the end he felt he could only be himself. The trip to India made a great impression on him, for he felt how ancient the country had remained, and how there was 'religiosity' everywhere: it put him in touch with the gods. But it was not until near the end of the English-speaking tour, in Glasgow, that Mezzogiorno relaxed and felt at one with Arjuna. The whole of *The Mahabharata*, he believed, had been a deep philosophical experience. 'Peter lets you do a kind of work on yourself, a research of yourself which goes in the direction of knowing yourself. I know that I am searching for myself and to work in this experience has been very important.'

Miriam Goldschmidt (Kunti), a West German national, read Brook's book *The Empty Space,* sold her late mother's wedding-ring and bought a one-way ticket to Paris, where she insisted on becoming a founder member of the Centre. An intense actress, she projects, off-stage, a complete lack of inhibition about her feelings of enthusiasm towards Brook. Married to the Swiss actor, Urs Bihler (Dushassana), she has one son and one daughter both of whom have Brook as godfather: he often visits their home, chatting to them in a smattering of different languages and will sit down and play old Russian folk songs on the piano. Paradoxically, Goldschmidt has a more combative, iconoclastic attitude to Brook than most, believing he can often be his own worst enemy, and that at times he is too dilatory and refuses to confront the problems which need to be tackled. During the New York run of *The Mahabharata*, for example, there was, according to her, a great deal of dissatisfaction among the cast, but all Brook would do – 'sitting there helpless and not able to give an excuse' – was to repeat to them, 'It's not the time.'

Vittorio Mezzogiorno

Miriam Goldschmidt and Urs Bihler were critical, too, of the text and characters in *The Mahabharata*. Bihler found Krishna had no unity, that he was different characters put together: 'At the centre there is no real playwright.' Both felt there were a lot of questions selfishly left unanswered in the text. Bihler, a small, bear-like actor of intelligence and power, with a deeply lined forehead, questioned why the goodness was 'so flatly left and so much space given to the bad characters'.

Bernard Shaw would have answered that the devil has all the best tunes. Brook's dramatic instincts overrode considerations of personal responsibility, but not of psychological complexity, especially with Karna, whom many of the actors tended to view with a certain envy, as having a definite tragic destiny. Jeffrey Kissoon pointed out that, 'He *is* the psychological character in the play.' This dimension, and the depth of his evil, was given to him by his ignorance of his background – he does not know who he is, and yet he has made so many commitments.

Like Bihler, Kissoon expressed doubts about *The Mahabharata*. Kissoon's father in Trinidad had been a practising Hindu, a holy man. Kissoon, who is British by nationality, has had a guru – a Hindu guide or spiritual teacher (in Sanskrit, he explains, guru means heavy or weighty). He declared himself unsatisfied on two counts, first that the ideal of the international group was not fully realised, and that they somehow never became unified. 'We evaded the issue of understanding', and never got through to answering the question ' "What is the purpose of your life?" If Brook would listen more; if

Dioume

every individual gave what he had . . .' In other words, they failed, off-stage, to develop a spiritual connection with one another. Second, he believed that ultimately the text was unsatisfactory because, in the original *Mahabharata,* all the stories relate to the core, the *Gita,* which is, as the Indian scholar K. M. Munshi pointed out, 'the noblest of scriptures and the grandest of sagas, the climax of which is reached in the wondrous Apocalypse of the Eleventh Canto'. This is condensed to two pages of printed text in Brook's version.

'What is the super-objective of this play?' Kissoon asked. 'It could never be answered.'

Instead of these ultimate, perhaps unattainable, satisfactions Kissoon claimed he had faith in something else – 'Faith in Peter'. He was 'the master above us all'. He had faith in the production because Brook knew how the theatre worked. Kissoon found the work very strenuous, and 'You tried to get rid of all the things you tried to hang on to before, to make you as close to *you* as possible so that "Nothing can touch the life that informs you"'.' Brook understood 'what puts bums on seats'.

Nearest the gods – or at least heroes – in real-life dimensions, the Senegalese actor, Mamadou Dioume, seemed to have no great difficulty with his mammoth and unforgettable Bhima, son of Kunti and of Vayu, the god of the wind – and 'the strongest man in the world'. But, unlike Bhima, Dioume is a pacifist, a Sunni Moslem who stated that war was never necessary. 'The *Koran* has never taught killing people and before he left this world the prophet said, "The only war is fighting oneself".'

Dioume found himself, however, very tense in the beginning. But when they went to India and he saw that 'All that they do was done simply . . . close to the earth, to the sky,' he started to view the world with another eye. 'I saw poverty but people enjoyed themselves. I went to temples, Shiva's Temple, and Vishnu's Temple. I talked to priests. What they told me was amazing. This is the only point. We must look beyond ourselves, look for knowledge to strengthen our beliefs.'

When you watch Dioume act, you experience how inadequate life is when lived only through the intellect. He acted Bhima with a powerful sense of deity, and his responses were unclouded by stifling concepts of the mind. Dioume's acting breaks down the barrier between the visible and the invisible. That the supremely intellectual Brook should respond to such direct simplicity is a measure of his belief that modern Western man has lost touch with myth and nature.

But Dioume had his problems long after they had been to India, and well into the period of rehearsal. 'Mamadou,' Brook said to him, 'would it be possible for you to go back through your own culture and find out who you are?' He did as he was told: he consulted members of his family, the folklore and religion of his country, its politics, everything which might have a bearing on the problem. It worked. The single note Brook constantly gave him later was, 'Enjoy yourself as much as you can.'

Trying to capture the invisible, Brook never lost touch with common sense. The use of the story-teller, Vyasa, encouraged the spectator's belief, and this device extended into Vyasa having a child-companion to whom the whole story is told. As Brook said, 'The onlooker is a partner who must be forgotten and still constantly kept in mind.'

Antonin Stahly-Vishwanadan, a tall, twelve-year-old boy born in Paris of French–Indian parents, served continually as an affecting and touching point of identification for the audience. 'I learnt,' he told me, 'lots of things that I can't explain, fundamental things which are not explainable.' His father had taken him round India and had shown him 'Where the exile was, where the war was.' Antonin believed that watching the war was not very interesting; he liked the first part best, 'with all the fire'.

5

The world in a grain of sand

Why so large cost, having so short a lease,
Dost thou upon thy fading mansion spend?
WILLIAM SHAKESPEARE

Close attention to the finest points of detail was evident in every department of the production of *The Mahabharata*, but in no area was this dedication more strikingly adaptable and complex than in the design and the costumes.

The wardrobe mistress, Barbara Higgins, whose participation in *The Mahabharata* dated only from early 1988, found herself amused by her trip to India, but not of the same awed spirit as the others: 'There is no spiritual atmosphere,' she declared iconoclastically, 'just poverty and inefficiency. I get very cross with religion.'

Most of the cast had greatly approved of India. On the twelve-day trip, Georges Corraface, horrified as he was at the Bombay slums, was surprised to find a positive quality: they were an eye-opener but not so pathetic and passive as he had been led to believe. 'Active misery, life was so strong in thin bodies . . .'

But Mireille Maalouf echoed Barbara Higgins and found herself angry at all the poverty, considering it as 'the bad influence of Hinduism'. The folkloric fervour did not impress her either, 'I am more touched by silence.'

Barbara Higgins at work in Joinville

Barbara Higgins had to take out to Delhi the fabric which Chloe Obolensky, the designer, and Pippa Cleator, her assistant, had had woven in Tunis, and have it shrunk. 'There was no water, so it was a difficult problem. Everything in the workshop was going to be better when the air-conditioning went on.' Which it never did. But they shrank the fabric finally in hot water in big bowls from a wonderful shop with a little old man in his seventies who had a hearing-aid. 'He always had dye of a certain colour – say oatmeal – all over one side of his head where he kept banging the deaf-aid with his hand to make it work. Monkeys crashed around outside, and in and out of the broken windows.'

In fact they had used six different workshops at various times: Pippa Cleator darted about on a scooter while the temperature hit 47°C; and not only was there a water crisis, but an electricity shortage too. Her particular interest was the fabrics – bought for the war coats in Tripoli and made of an oily, rough-woven goat's wool.

Chloe Obolensky, born in Athens of Greek parents and educated in France and England – she was married to a Russian – not only designed the basic sets for all the different venues where *The Mahabharata* was played, but she also, in most cases of the tour, redesigned or refurbished the spaces or interiors to accommodate *The Mahabharata*'s staging needs. She also originated all the basic props. 'She is the real star of this show,' Brook had asserted affectionately, and he meant it.

The task was of mammoth proportions, and unlike the acting or

the writing it could not be evolved with the same sense of leisure and calm. 'Luxury, today, is time,' Obolensky noted sagely. Her first collaboration with Brook had been on *The Cherry Orchard* and she followed this with costume designs for the different versions of *Carmen*. For four years preceding her association with Brook she researched and wrote the magnificently documented *The Russian Empire: a Portrait in Photographs,* and, beginning work on *The Mahabharata* and travelling to India with Carrière and Brook, she began to build up a massive dossier of photographs and drawings more or less at once.

She told me about the trip in the props room at Joinville:

> I decided not to read the script beforehand. I hadn't been to India before. It's halfway to the Orient. I wanted to take in what's around – see what Peter reacts to, what I react to myself. It was a startling experience. I knew we were doing it at the Bouffes and I knew I didn't want to decorate, but to create an atmosphere to make it possible for actors to tell a story, which meant putting in those elements most suggestive both for the actors and the audience.

Obolensky is Brook's definition of a true theatre designer, in other words someone who thinks of design as being all the time in motion, in action, in relation to what the actor brings to a scene as it unfolds:

Unlike the easel painter, in two dimensions, or the sculptor in three, the designer thinks in terms of the fourth dimension, the passage of time – not the stage picture, but the stage moving picture. A film editor shapes his material after the event: the stage designer is often like the editor of an Alice-Through-the-Looking-Glass film, cutting dynamic material in shapes, before this material has yet come into being. The later he makes his decisions, the better.

The later she makes her decisions . . . For a long time before the French stage version opened, she puzzled how to adapt the Bouffes to *The Mahabharata*: at first anything was possible, and at the beginning she thought of an uneven stage floor, constructed with valleys which had little walks. But finally she realised that the walls of the theatre were the key to any scenic arrangement, and that she would have to close all windows and doors to block out any decorative elements and to achieve a sober atmosphere.

'I work on instinct, images, emotions, impressions. I suddenly realised what it was prompted me in the direction my design took. It's the memory at twilight of our first evening in Benares. We had just been out on a boat and we were sitting on the *ghats* where the bodies were burned. I was looking up at the sheer buildings, the walls on the waterfront – I could have been in an Italian medieval city. In the dark we feel the volumes and don't see the details. At the origin of the work was this darkness. The space came naturally.'

Next they had to find a basic colour: for a moment Brook toyed with a white background and Obolensky also thought white a pure aesthetic proposition, but then both decided white looked sad. They chose a reddish – 'red-ochre' – warm space in the end, and reworked the walls of the theatre for a whole month, adding more Indian-red and yellow-ochre to make the colour mount in intensity, at the same time ensuring the unity of the place was preserved and that all separation between playing space and auditorium disappeared.

The ground was the consideration that came after the space, and they settled on earth for this: 'beaten, desiccated' earth, an Indian element which fused perfectly with the Bouffes. 'Then water arrived, for one thing calls up another. When you have the earth, next water, then fire follows. These three elements allied to the architecture of the theatre have a capacity of evocation so great that they are enough in themselves.'

So the Bouffes was stripped down to a spartan, childlike simplicity, and they had a visual 'language' or 'constellation' which could travel elsewhere and be instantly accessible to every nationality. It was the equivalent of Carrière's basic vocabulary, creating as wide an appeal as possible, and it became, of course, easily available to different audiences wherever the production travelled. In Glasgow, for instance, the cobbles of the old transport museum disappeared under 240 tons of thick and hardened clay, quarried in Greenock. In Avignon, Adelaide and Perth it actually played in quarries; yet for Obolensky, when it came to filming the work the Bouffes remained 'the golden rule – classical yet entirely original – the scale of what goes on is always right'.

Draupadi as shadow puppet

'It is easy,' said Brook, 'to spoil an actor's performance with the wrong costume.' If the space had a discreet rapport with India, the costumes had a much greater power of affirmation of Hindu culture. Obolensky recalled several formative episodes from her trips to India which inspired her: a sacred spring near Madurai, high up on a hill, with a little temple dominating it where whole families went to bathe, play with water, sit around to eat; two boys of ten or twelve, the younger making up the other, in silence, pushing colour through a powder tube to fashion a design in the forehead of his friend with precise concentration; in Benares, coming back late from the Ganges, the explosion of a nocturnal marriage, lit by sparks from a generator, the bride and groom posing with crowns of flowers; then walking across New Delhi at five in the morning, with people everywhere lighting the first fire of the morning; in South India a march in the dark night where they celebrated the spirit of a dead hero . . .

All these experiences helped to inform the designer from within; and give her a strong sense of Indian identity. But she avoided three traps – folk imitation, re-interpretation, and disguise. She preferred to study authentic cuts of historic Indian clothes in the Musée de L'Homme in Paris, in London's Victoria and Albert Museum, in Benares or in the Calico Textile Museum of Ahmedabad, in order to find the exceptional images which transcended the temporal. In such a way Obolensky found shapes which existed in antiquity and which could still exist today. As she said, 'It would have been ridiculous to disguise Poles or Irishmen as Indians, for an Indian body is very different from a Polish or an Irish body. We had so many different physical types . . . in a sense as soon as you put people in costume you're saying something . . .'

She stressed that there is not a single 'cut' which is not taken from an original. Basically she looked for archetypal shapes – long pleated trousers, long hose, eighteenth-century shapes evocative of colonial India – emphasising the geometric simplicity. 'Non-Asians do not look right in loose, unstitched clothing,' so the costumes were generally very bold and sculpted – 'You always have to exaggerate so that the volume comes across.' Mallika Sarabhai paid tribute to the subtle achievement in using India's great wealth in craft and combining all the basic elements, 'mixing over the centuries and across regions'.

The costumes for the war changed three times. Dr Jyotindra Jain, the director of the Crafts Museum of Delhi told her 'you can learn it all in three books and five trips'. But, says Obolensky, 'doing things in theory, then putting it to the test, it becomes yours.' Four and a half years have made *The Mahabharata* hers, for 'little by little you are freed of this and that, and can improve in a real way, and it gives you stamina to change things'. As for Brook, she calls their work 'a very close collaboration: very often we have the same instinct and simple sympathy of taste'.

Obolensky and Pippa Cleator also originated all the props, many of them again very basic; mats, earthen pots, flowers, lamps – or simple pieces of cloth which can perform many functions. Tied up, a cloth can carry possessions or it can cover a body, be a baby's winding-sheet, serve as a table cloth, hang on a wall as a decoration. Flowers made their own ambience, either in garlands, or by being strewn over floors, the intention always being to evoke rather than to illustrate.

The exquisite, inlaid-patterned dice table, for the game on which the whole play turns, evolved first from a standard Indian dice game fabric, a patchwork which players would lay out after pulling back the carpet. But Brook liked the idea of the noise of the dice crashing on something wooden, and so they fashioned a board: but then it needed

**Nineteenth-century illustrations
from the *Bhagavad Gita*
*(The British Library)***

to be put on legs – the first pattern in the shape of a cross was also retained. Finally after experimenting with plywood on bricks they found a model of a Rajasthani table, and, having it specially made with inlaid wood, they adapted the dice configuration to this.

Props and acting business sometimes developed together, one rendering the other redundant. For the birth of Duryodhana they first considered it realistic to have him bursting out of a big earthenware pot. They made a big pot, with the idea that it would be broken nightly and remade. But, said Pippa Cleator, 'it got wheeled off again in a space of minutes. In the end Duryodhana himself rolled in, in the shape of a big ball.' Likewise with Krishna's disk. 'We wanted something real, like those Chakra disks which gave sparks and fire from ball-bearings rubbing together.' But finally there was nothing. 'Krishna's gesture with sound plus the movement of the actor himself proved much more vivid than any electrical equipment.'

As well as the props and costumes, the designers also had to restructure or adapt the space inside each of the foreign tour venues. In Zürich they played in the huge boat-repair shed on the edge of the lake. It had sixty-foot roller-shutter doors at the lake end which shut out the light (the stage was at the lake end of the shed). In the final moments of the opening marathon performance at seven a.m., when all that miraculous and powerful lighting, originally designed by Jean Kalman, came up for 'Paradise', they silently opened the end doors and there, perfectly framed behind the cast, the rising sun flooded the shed with golden light and stunned the audience's vision.

If this was an effect Obolensky and Cleator could not exactly prepare for, they certainly utilised all the natural circumstances to the best possible advantage. For Obolensky Los Angeles was the least satisfactory place of all: the newly constructed Raleigh Studio Theater had been badly finished, and Obolensky chose to put up with a 'constructor's artificial idea which I relit with a red transparent haze'.

In New York the Majestic Theater appeared on the surface to be an American relative of the Bouffes du Nord. It had been abandoned for twenty-five or thirty years – there were 'beautiful things in stucco, old and patina'd, it really had an atmosphere'. They restored some of the boxes, taking the predominant red of the boxes around the sides and back to link the back wall with the auditorium. 'I was astonished,' observed Obolensky, 'to find articles saying we had come to "distress" the theatre and give it an old-fashioned look.'

The quarries at Adelaide and Perth (as at Athens and Avignon for the French production) offered her only limited scope for landscaping or adaptation of setting. But there were again the larger possibilities that nature could appear to have been directed by Brook. But the open-space venues remained for Obolensky the touchstone –

still together with Les Bouffes – when it came to planning the film. Open-air performance had also always been Brook's ideal.

In the former gasworks at Copenhagen Obolensky used 'all the rust stains. I glazed the entire surface with warm transparent sienna'. In Glasgow she went into 'radical transformation of what was there'. To convert the Old Transport Museum took nearly four months and cost £100,000. Obolensky insisted that the walls, coated in flaking magnolia paint, should be sand-blasted so that they had a natural surface like Les Bouffes. She then built three walls, including a back one, so that the space came fully alive. Both she and Brook had, they later realised, gravitated towards choosing industrial buildings of the nineteenth century. 'A functional place is architecturally noble,' said Brook at the Copenhagen press conference, 'because of some curious quality in nineteenth century architects which made them give their best to those buildings.' Presumably this came from their belief in divinity, if only, as we now see it, allied to progress and Mammon.

In the end the Glasgow *Mahabharata* cost only £325,000, making it the cheapest on the world circuit. In Japan, at the Ginza Saison Theatre, the play had its most conventional, proscenium arch presentation, but even here the elemental factors of the scene – air, earth, fire and water – came over as dominant images.

With the film of *The Mahabharata,* Obolensky had to progress even more into realms of suggestibility, if not of full realism. According to Cleator, Brook was always playing in an unreal setting to give a feeling of reality. But on screen not everything could be placed on the actor, for example for the second part 'Exile in the Forest' there would have to be some suggestion of a forest. This was ultimately conveyed by tall reeds, shot in such a way that they seemed to extend indefinitely – on stage there was no need for any marked sylvan aspect. They also had to change the costumes fundamentally: 'On stage you can put contrasting colours together, but on film with too much delineation between colours it becomes confusing.'

Obolensky identified the main problem as 'How to produce a film with the same economy of elements as on the stage, and not to come out with a poor image.' The eye would never take in the complexity and richness of all it had seen on stage, so they had to 'decompose' the play and select images and backgrounds which would give an impressionistic feeling to the action, like the hazy background of a portrait. While in the small studio they would be 'always up against one wall or another', and so the regulation of lighting became of paramount importance, in order to find 'within one space so many different moods'.

After a little time filming they realised that walls and details could not lovingly be dwelt on, and what presented a particular difficulty was to fit a lot of people into one composition – for example the dice game. But the greatest problem of all would be to find time, for Obolensky refused to use preconceived ideas arrived at by means of a story-board. 'A man who does lighting has to take time,' she insisted. It became 'a race to take time'.

One paradox emerged from filming the war. While it became enormously reduced in complexity from the stage and as a result more practical, the number of those taking part had to be dramatically increased – the leaders of the armies could no longer be seen as doing all their own fighting! The quilted tops and breastplates had to be made more elaborate, and the effect made everyone appear more tribal.

Music was an extremely active ingredient of *The Mahabharata*, both on the stage and on screen. In the theatrical version its function was recognisably oriental, with the musicians present, visible, incorporated in the spectacle – a full participation, with the music almost engaged in dialogue with the action, providing an unending commentary and mood-regulator. For nine hours of playing time, Brook saw from the start the need for infinite variety in the music, and sought at first a composer of the calibre of Richard Peaslee – someone as important to the music as Jean-Claude Carrière was important to the text: 'A superspecialist in his field and totally inside what he did'.

But of course the music also had to be oriental, and although Brook interviewed and listened to Middle Eastern and Indian composers, he failed to find one who could serve the needs of a Western audience, or go further than proposing 'something which came naturally from improvised music'. Finally he settled for the Japanese musician Toshi Tsuchitori, a friend of Yoshi Oida, who had begun by learning traditional Japanese drums as a child, and had then become a master of improvisation. Tsuchitori had already provided the music for CIRT's productions of *Ubu,* and *Conference of the Birds,* and well versed in the research methods of the group he had explored ethnic music in the course of trips to Africa, Asia, and the Middle East. He had even ventured into the field of prehistoric music, reconstructing it for recordings using stones and bronze bells as instruments.

Work on the music began in 1980. Brook and Tsuchitori decided that improvisation, not written music, was desirable and that diverse sources should be explored – similar to the casting of the players. The musician voyaged far – to India, where he spent two years collecting folk music largely on foot – to Nepal, Sri Lanka, Bali, Indonesia, also to Africa and America. He studied local music in all these places, bought the indigenous instruments, met the musicians.

One year before performances began, they organised actor–musician workshops with fifteen instrumentalists from all parts: 'At this stage,' said Tsuchitori, 'it was impossible to improvise together – everyone could only play his own music. But the confrontation of all these materials was fruitful.' Little by little Brook defined the colours he wanted, and chose instruments. Then actors and musicians improvised together on texts, so as to forge a relationship, a state of 'shared spirit'.

The group that finally came together consisted of Djamchid Chemirani and Mahmoud Tabrizi-Zadeh, Iranians; Kudsi Erguner, Turkish; and Kim Menzer, a Dane introduced to Brook by the Indian violinist, Subramaniam, musical adviser to the French production. Brook had wanted one European musician, so he dispatched Menzer to Madras to play the South Indian oboe or 'nagaswaram'. He also learnt to play the shanai (West Bengal pipe), launeddas (Sardinian clarinet), fujara, conch and didjeridoo (Aborigine pipe). Tsuchitori and Chemirani both played roughly thirty percussion instruments. Erguner, a Sufi musician, just played the ney (flute), while the Iranian

Tabrizi-Zadeh, who teaches music at the Sorbonne, could manage four or more kinds of kamantche – Iranian or Indian violins – and a Turkish *tambour à archet*. The rhythm of the music, Tabrizi-Zadeh said, always had to be predetermined and fixed, with perhaps three or four recognisable melodies 'sufficiently clearly fixed'.

One great problem, Tsuchitori remembered, was to 'verify or modify the tension of the drum skins in relation to the humidity or dryness of the air. In Avignon, in the open air, I had to heat them up several times in front of a radiator – without forgetting to play, to sing (during the game of dice) and concentrate.' To employ at any point the classic Indian instrument, the sitar, Brook told him, would make the audience think immediately of Ravi-Shankar.

Except for the music played during the *Bhagavad Gita,* a composition by Subramaniam, the music remained improvised – but the dramatic moments were always fixed. 'The musical reference,' said Tsuchitori, 'is Indian, but in their application the diversity of instruments we employ lose their cultural connotations.'

6

Begging, grafting, stealing, wheedling

If we do not wish to go backwards, we must run.
PELAGIUS

The search for forty million francs to film *The Mahabharata* was no less an epic than the work itself. It, too, had an international cast which included the Rockefeller Foundation, an English lord, Yves Saint-Laurent International, Indian Sanskrit scholars, musicologists, Hollywood moguls, the City of Zürich, the *Sun* newspaper, the Mayor of Copenhagen, the Handicrafts and Handlooms Export Corporation of India, Tripoli accountants, Bombay taxi-drivers and Glasgow traffic supervisors. The quest for the right location or studios lasted nearly three years. England, Australia, Denmark, Mexico, Greece, Tunisia, Hungary, Japan, Egypt, Poland, Yugoslavia and The Canaries were all at one time or other considered. Two serious attempts were made to film in India. It is not surprising that sometimes the actors felt their fate was that of being dangled from the tooth of some international corporate monster: Mahabharata Inc. or Ltd. or *Société Anonyme.*

One evening in October 1988, in the Tour d'Argent Brasserie at the Bastille, near his Paris flat, Brook recounted to me the whole story. It began as far back as 1982 when Michael Kustow, formerly director of London's Institute of Contemporary Arts, and then head of Channel 4 Television arts programmes, had put down £50,000 as co-producer of the original French version. It then moved swiftly on to the first night at Avignon on 7 July 1985: in the Boulbon quarry audience sat Kustow. He had come to see how his investment had turned out. Flamboyant and didactic, Kustow had once worked with the avant-garde director Roger Planchon, and spoke fluent French. Stunned by the performance Kustow knew the time had really arrived to develop *The Mahabharata* as a television or feature film. He already had the option for his company to broadcast it in Britain. He started looking for producers and immediately sent two off to Brook to formulate plans to shoot it.

Right after the Avignon opening Brook also had a call from Australia. The Bicentennial Authority wanted the production for the Perth and Adelaide Festivals in 1988 – in English. News of the success travelled quickly to New York, where Harvey Lichtenstein, an old friend and collaborator of Brook's, and head of the Brooklyn Academy of Music, also wanted an English version for his theatre festival in 1987. William Wilkinson, organising genius of Brook's world tour of *A Midsummer Night's Dream*, said it had to be done in English and that he would mount the tour. He would find a London venue where it would have its première. The Los Angeles Festival was also interested. So was the City of Zürich . . .

Brook, now with potential commitments to keep *The Mahabharata* alive until early 1988, decided that the 'hypothetical market', as he called it, for a film must be realised. It could have a crucial effect, too, by providing financial support, in actually keeping the tour going. He never saw at the time how many years it would take.

Next it became the turn of Joseph Strick, veteran Hollywood producer, to enter the story. Strick had to his credit an honourable list of high-brow films such as the adaptation of James Joyce's *Ulysses*. His company had pioneered a system of booking non-commercial but prestigious films into cinemas all over the United States for short runs, and by means of concentrated advertising, had raised modest box-office profits on them. Strick 'excited us all in his scheme', said Brook. He did not want to direct, he wanted to raise $4 million – 'it looked very sensible' – including half a million from Channel 4, a million from his own sources, and a million from the Brooklyn Academy of Music.

For his own contribution, he and Brook made a list of fifty notable American backers and producers – such as the Presidents of Universal Pictures, Columbia and Orion films – sending each a telegram asking for support. 'Nine-tenths didn't reply, and when we did get an answer it was usually from someone like the office-boy in Toulouse,' observed Brook.

It was back to zero. *The Mahabharata*, playing in French, had swiftly visited Italy, Greece, Spain, and West Germany, and had now become firmly entrenched in the Bouffes du Nord for the winter of 1985-6. As well as Australia and New York, Los Angeles had become a firm date, Switzerland and now India were now distinct hopes, Tokyo a more distant possibility. Brook, never happy with his actors simply running in a show, was keen to arrange something extra for them to do – such as taking part in a community project, or performing improvisations. He had always been bombarded by the public with requests to be allowed to see the work of CIRT – especially to watch rehearsals. He and Marie-Hélène Estienne arranged an 'open house' and invited 400 young professionals to a two-week workshop. Brook would give a talk and explain their work: they could do exercises, intensively rehearse a scene from *The Cherry Orchard*, and so on.

The result, called by Brook 'a very rewarding and emotional experience', became the subject for an R.T.F. film made by Jean-Claude Lubtchansky. While shooting his footage, Lubtchansky asked Brook if he could film some of *The Mahabharata* for the programme.

Brook agreed, and Jean-Claude's brother, Willy, a distinguished cameraman, filmed the nine hours of a marathon at the Bouffes du Nord.

In the meantime new moves had begun on the big motion picture front. The – according to Brook – 'brilliantly intuitive' David Picker, David Puttnam's producer for Universal Artists, stepped in with plans to make a full-scale feature – a 'project of power and imagination'.

Kustow flew to Paris, where he and Picker dined with Brook and Jean-Claude Carrière. The budget expanded to $12 or 13 million for a single feature, to be shot on location in India. A script would have to be ready by the end of the Los Angeles visit. Carrière haggled over length; he felt that they could not tell the essence of the story in two and three-quarter hours.

Brook found he left the dinner feeling the project was in danger of falling between two stools. Shooting in India with real elephants and – of necessity – international stars, meant 'We could be, in a sense, pulling down the level of imagination of the theatre version. You would need millions of fireflies for the battle at night, and a thousand elephants':

> The army lights up the thousands and thousands of flames. The shining rises from the earth. It's as though the trees of a forest were covered with glittering flies.

'Once you have a landscape you have to fill it,' Michael Birkett, producer of Brook's films of *The Marat-Sade* and *King Lear*, agreed later.

At this moment Brook recalled Willy Lubtchansky and the nine hours of film this fiery-looking, dark-haired French Pole had shot at the Bouffes du Nord. 'I had a dynamic idea, possibly a revolutionary idea of shooting a film,' Brook told me. 'With the English version

now definitely in preparation, we were planning twenty marathon performances in India, all of them outdoors. Why not take Lubtchansky with us and film every marathon?'

This plan further envisaged a computer that, from day to day, would work out which angles of performances had not been covered, and progressively make sure that, by the end, absolutely nothing had been left out. They would keep ten days spare at the end of the tour to shoot, in an empty, open-air theatre, additional scenes.

Brook loved the whole idea. 'We would be dynamically sculpting it and developing it as we go along.' Moreover, with the dramatic and colourful participation of thousands of Indians piled round cliffs – their reactions intercut with the spectacle itself – it could well have become a happening of much wider consequences. 'India being brought back to India,' proclaimed Brook triumphantly. ('It would have been the editing job of the century,' Birkett commented later.)

Bright-eyed and bushy-tailed, Brook rushed off to Jeremy Isaacs, then Head of Channel 4, and gained his enthusiastic support for the whole innovative notion. But, ominously, the booking for *The Mahabharata*'s Indian tour had not yet come through. If the play itself never got to India, how could the film be made there?

In the early months of 1986 Brook had lunch with French Prime Minister, Jacques Chirac. The French *Mahabharata*, first presented with French and Indian government sponsors at Avignon under the banner of the 'Festival of India', had already given a prestigious fillip to Franco-Indian relations. But Brook and his partners were finding it increasingly hard going to mount an Indian tour: the technical and financial problems seemed insuperable. Above all they could not discover the right Indian, perhaps highly placed in ruling or cultural circles, to pull all the threads together. They had heard that there was another festival year coming up – the anniversary of Nehru's birth.

Brook told Chirac the whole problem. He fixed the Prime Minister with his 'twinkling ice-pick' eyes. 'It can all be solved if the French send *The Mahabharata* as a present to India for the Nehru festival.'

The proposal was audacious. France had already given Brook five million francs for *The Mahabharata*. But Chirac was sympathetic and embraced it. 'I will send a telex at once to my Ambassador,' he told Brook. A few days later Brook himself flew to Delhi.

The company's negotiations here were not progressing well. The country was in a constant state of political crisis. Any government body or person trying to raise money for the tour risked charges of encouraging a 'lay, even immoral attitude to Hinduism'; strong 'segments' of government, according to one well-placed Indian source, wrote off the whole *Mahabharata* project as 'foreign and white and élitist'.

Even the distinguished writer Shanta Serbjeet Singh, who praised the Avignon production in the *Indian Express* and called it 'the most important interpolation, interpretation and interposition between two vastly different cultures, that of the East and West, since the original was written', had qualified his enthusiasm with, 'The difference between it and what I can get from even the most modest mono-*Mahabharata* of Teeian Bai is the difference between *bhet-puri* and the humblest *prasad* from a sacred shrine.' Brook's *Mahabharata*, predicted Singh, would touch a much deeper nerve centre in the Western psyche than in the Eastern.

But if official India could not be stirred, Brook still had a trump card to play: Chirac's telex. He proceeded to the French Embassy in Delhi, but found no trace of the telex's arrival. 'The French Ambassador there was very hostile to our problem.' Little did that Ambassador know that, in the long term, he was performing a valuable service to his country.

They decided to postpone India, but in the four or five months of intense activity that preceded the clinching of the deal for the English tour the idea of the film was far from being dropped. 'We now move to spring 1987', Brook continued his account. 'Rehearsals had begun, and a film option had been written into the contract of each member of the English-speaking cast. 'There were still two interested parties: Britain's Channel 4 and the Brooklyn Academy of Music. 'Both had raised their commitment to a million dollars each, but together this was not enough for even the most moderately budgeted television mini-series.'

Kustow approached Reiner Moritz, who ran the international film and video distribution company RM Associates, based in London and New York. Brook, hearing of the abolition of London's

Reiner Moritz *(Photograph by Guido Mangold)*

Greater London Council, rang its Director of Recreation and Arts, his former producer Michael Birkett. Son of a famous lawyer, Birkett was a member of the House of Lords. 'Now that you're free,' Brook told him, 'this is the call to action. I need someone to organise the film of *The Mahabharata*.' Birkett, in spite of numerous other public appointments, responded at once: 'I recognised,' he told me later, 'that this was a Brook big public number, potentially a major movie.'

Next all interested parties flew to Paris. On Micheline Rozan's shrewd suggestion Brook arranged a public dress rehearsal of the English version, split into two parts, and shown over two days, just for the purpose of raising money for the film. Moritz, recording Herbert von Karajan's *Don Giovanni* at the Salzburg Festival, could not come for the first part. He sent his nineteen-year-old son. 'I thought this one of the Kustow extravaganzas,' he said, 'and I was prepared to kill it!'

The dress rehearsal nearly never took place. Georges Corraface, the French-Greek actor who had been re-cast in the crucial role of Duryodhana, fell gravely ill, while Urs Bihler, who replaced Corraface, tore some cartilage and had to enter hospital for an operation. 'We had to face a crucial run-through with two understudies. This was an immensely dramatic moment,' Brook recalled. 'What should we do? Should we call it off?'

On Rozan's advice they went through with it. 'In the event,' commented Brook, 'enough confidence reigned at our meeting in a hotel suite next morning for everyone to be convinced.' He was being modest. Reiner Moritz remembered later that the only thing he said over dinner to Colin Leventhal, financial controller of Channel 4, was 'Where do we find the money?' He, for one, was prepared to use his contacts to try and raise over one and a half million dollars from television sales outside Britain and the United States, a seemingly impossible task.

In the event he did just that. RM Associates negotiated sales to some twenty-one different countries. Moritz's first contract, amazingly, came from Catholic monarchist Spain, for an unexpected $300,000. The German-speaking countries and Australia followed quickly, to the joint tune of $600,000. Moritz also achieved the feat of selling *The Mahabharata* to all five Scandinavian countries: 'unique', he believed, especially with the inclusion of Iceland. This puzzled him until he realised that Icelanders 'thrived on great epics by the fireplace . . . cosmogonic sagas are understood commonly, they touch so many things in human beings'. Finally, a complicated deal with Indian television committed India to spending $80,000 on costumes and artefacts which would all be made inside India.

The protean *Mahabharata* film project – perhaps a hero taking many forms to survive – was now more firmly envisaged as a conventional mini-series boiled down to six hours. It would be shot on location in Australia, at the end of the English tour. Brook liked the idea of a quarry, which 'would preserve the epic quality and provide intimacy,' he told his audience in an eloquent speech. They were booked to play in the Perth and Adelaide quarries. They would shoot specifically for television from a prepared script, without an audience, and take ten weeks. Brook was again demonstrating to himself, and to those in his closest circle, that there were no hard and fast rules. 'While the interest of India and the Indian context was great,' he said to me later, 'I believe in always adapting everything to the available conditions.'

There was already a big difficulty in this new plan. While *The Mahabharata*, after its ecstatically received English première in Zürich, was winging its way to New York via Los Angeles, Harvey Lichtenstein could still not be sure of his million dollars until they knew the outcome of a crucial meeting due to be held in New York on November 15. As the production was opening at the Majestic on 13 October, they could not afford to wait so long. The company, engaged only until March 1988, would be disbanded immediately after the last night in Adelaide. They had to have the film prepared for shooting at the very latest in April.

Brook sent Birkett to Australia to try and raise money locally, but this was a complete disaster. 'Michael went all around the hard-nosed Aussies who said, "What's in it for us?" We had to face the fact that we would not get a cent.'

Yet again the full amount of money eluded them. The cast was told by William Wilkinson, 'We can give you no guarantee, but we would like an option for filming for twelve further weeks in Adelaide or Perth'. The make-or-break date was 15 November 1987. As Bill Wilkinson described it, 'The begging, grafting, stealing, wheedling', had to go on.

Like Channel Four the Brooklyn Academy of Music had been one of the original producers of *The Mahabharata*. Harvey Lichtenstein, 'arguably an American Diaghilev' said Kustow, had been brought in to the project by Kustow, and had involved the Corporation for Public Broadcasting who had already contributed $75,000. Most of this had been squandered on hiring extra staff to fill out large wodges of paper for grants – or on legal staff or 'development directors' dispatched to Europe by Concorde.

The thirty-page document for raising the money in America had originally envisaged production beginning in Australia in March. The first US airdate would have been in spring 1989. With typical American overkill – and because they were appealing for money from public-minded bodies such as the Rockefeller Foundation, the Ford

Foundation, and the National Endowment for the Arts – the document listed eminent scholars whom Brook and Carrière had consulted during the twelve years they had already spent on the project. These included the French Sanskritist Madeleine Biardeau; Alf Hiltebield, American Hindu scholar; Barbara Stoler Miller, translator of the *Bhagavad Gita*, Kapila Vatsayana, Indian Theatre scholar, and so on. 'They would only do it if enough pundits could be found to recommend it,' said Brook.

None of these eminences could, however, shift the basic inertia or unwillingness of the Americans to give any quick assent to funding the project, and when, in the middle of November, all the interested parties assembled in New York in Harvey Lichtenstein's office, they were told that one of the major foundations would not have its meeting until the following February. "Within a second the Aussie project was off," Brook commented.

Instead, there began a marathon to fill in further dates for the English company after Australia, with the hope that, in February 1988, the extra money necessary for the film would be approved and that the company would still be available. Sharp-tongued, but caring for her volatile *Mahabharata* family, Micheline Rozan took on herself the burden of guaranteeing salaries after the end of the Australian tour, to give some flexibility in organising the future. All kinds of new plans were floated to give the English tour new life: invitations to Mexico, to the Canary Islands, to Singapore, while an earlier idea of visiting Copenhagen with the French version which had never come to fruition, was eagerly reactivated.

William Wilkinson now sprang into a key role in the film's development. He revived an old ambition which, not from want of effort, had fallen by the wayside: to bring the play to England. He had already spent a year searching out a London venue, but none of the possibilities, which included the Customs House Building in Victoria and the *Sun* printing works in Stanford Street, had advanced beyond the preliminary stage, while the very negative attitude of the Department of the Environment had also dampened efforts. They had toyed with the Lyceum Theatre, with the Roundhouse, but neither had been in a performing condition. So one weekend they had dropped the whole idea of London for the English première – and given it to Zürich – at a price to the Swiss. One bank, the Union Bank of Switzerland, alone contributed £130,000. Wilkinson reckoned it cost on average half a million dollars to prepare each venue for *The Mahabharata*. Massive subsidy to cover this, air fares, and freight was a necessary pre-condition.

Wilkinson now scuttled round England for possible quarries to plug the gap: they looked at Kidlington, outside Oxford, next to the airport; at Leicester; at Maidstone quarry – too chalky for Brook's taste. Wilkinson even found a barn in Stratford from which he was prepared to remove the roof and rebuild it. But an increasing sense of desperation dogged him until one day, out of the blue, a man rang him from Wales. 'I'm just off to Scotland to take up a new post as deputy director of the Glasgow Festival and I heard you were looking for somewhere to do *The Mahabharata*.'

Neil Wallace was the man's name: he thought it an utter scandal Brook's work would not be seen in Britain. 'Here was this man's best work in forty years, it was *in English* and it was going everywhere except Britain.' Wallace set out to find ideal premises and after rejecting a ship's engine factory, started in 1903 by a German engineer called Diesel, he and Wilkinson agreed on the Old Transport Museum – the main obstacle here being the main road which ran alongside it, with heavy traffic night and day. 'We'll come to Glasgow provided you close the road,' stipulated Brook. The City Fathers complied.

The wilder schemes of Mexico and Korea were financially unrealisable but Copenhagen crystallised as the new saviour of *The Mahabharata* company and film. It now stepped in before Glasgow to fill the gap – while, after Glasgow, Tokyo had always been ready to host the production. Thus the protracted difficulties over finance for the film served to prolong the stage tour for at least six months – and brought the production to Britain.

With regard to the film Brook now found himself an exponent of completely controlled circumstances. 'We could do it in a British studio if we had the money.' But they did not have the money: they always seemed half a million short. Brook delivered a paper to the interested parties on his new concept: 'Stylised intimacy', he called it, based on the playing at the Bouffes du Nord. When he outlined his plans – taking, as he said, a certain delight in that he was advocating the complete opposite of what he had previously pleaded – those present could evaluate his very special kind of performance: indefatigable, tough and absolutely determined, but motionless, quiet-voiced and brimming with truth and freshness. He was playing his own game of dice against fate, determined that what seemed a set-back should ultimately grow to be an advantage.

So a new operation began – a quest for studios in cheaper countries, which brought them back again to India. After all, Brook pointed out, they made 800 films a year in India. He talked to Mallika Sarabhai, who grew very eloquent over the possibilities, while Marie-Hélène Estienne flew with Birkett to Madras, Bangalore, then Bombay. But none of the studios in the big cities had all the necessary facilities. For instance they found an air-conditioned studio in Madras, but no one could guarantee there would be no power cuts, and there were no private generators.

Brook joined them in Kerala, in South India, to inspect some
studios, after Harvey Lichtenstein phoned the good news, at four
a.m. one February morning, that the BAM money had come
through. Sarabhai believed that the resources of the Kaiah Ministry
for Culture were considerable, and that the minister himself had sent
his closest collaborator to Kerala. Brook described how after a
nightmare journey they drove out of this little town and found a
Sunset Boulevard where the studios stood behind noble portico gates
surrounded by trees. There was certainly a big 'stage', but Brook had
an impression that a few locals had been hurriedly assembled to give
the idea there were staff – while the processing laboratory had broken
down.

We need air-conditioning, Brook had said, but on the spot they
flatly answered no. Their reason? First, all films in India were made
on location and second, the studio rent was only a ridiculous fifty
pounds a day: with air-conditioning they would have to put up the
price. Conclusion: 'The death knell of this studio would be to
improve it.'

They also discovered the local government, prestige or no
prestige, was completely bankrupt. But this trip did yield one great
dividend: Bhaskar Ghose, from Doordarshan Television, joined the
project as a television co-producer: with India unable to export
rupees he pledged the $400,000 for costumes and artefacts which
would all be made in India and exported – but to where?

Next they explored Budapest and Zagreb: 'flirting with the
Eastern bloc'. Then it was Cairo's turn, this dismissed on account of
its unbearable heat in August (filming would now have to start after
Tokyo). Next they went to Athens, where they considered two
studios. The better of these had a permanent control-room which
they would have had to rent complete with eight video technicians.
Tunis came up next, with a studio built by Zeffirelli and Polanski, an
attractive proposition which again had the team examining all the
facilities, and being charmed by President Bourguiba's son-in-law,
who was extremely keen to make Tunis the new centre of European
Culture – like Rome or Madrid twenty years ago. They worked in
Tunis for several days, even brought over a production manager.
Before deciding they held a last dinner in Paris, at which Brook
noticed Willy Lubtchansky looking concerned: 'I'm worried that by
the time we've brought in the key technicians it will be as expensive
as London or Paris,' he told Brook. Although Tunis still remained
the favourite, Lubtchansky surreptitiously took Brook to see the old
Joinville studios out in the East of Paris that everyone had forgotten
about, and which were due to be demolished in a year. There were
many advantages in Joinville . . . much cheaper than the Bois de

A page from the numerous *Mahabharata* comics published in India

Boulogne studios: 'At least we thought we would be at home – home, of course, being where there is a mutual interest.'

Suddenly the Tunisian costs seemed to spiral: the French idea lifted off and Lubtchansky suggested an exceptionally bright and young producer, Michel Propper. Brook gave Propper – 'the right man with nerves – young, adventurous, aggressive, entrepreneurial", as Reiner Moritz called him – only a few days to submit a budget so that they could weigh up the two projects. They fixed crucial meetings at the Hotel Raphäel in the Avenue Kleber for a Friday in April 1988. If by that Friday they had not got a film, they would lose the wardrobe mistress, Barbara Higgins, due to leave shortly to supervise the making of the costumes in India.

The meeting with the Tunisians was fixed for eleven a.m., that with Propper for two thirty p.m. But at ten in the morning the Tunisians phoned from Rome to say there was an Air France strike at Rome, and that they would not be arriving until the early evening. Right, said Brook, we can reverse the appointments.

Here again, commented Brook, Micheline Rozan had the right instinct at a crucial moment; she called up Air France and asked if any flights were delayed. The answer was no. 'Suddenly the glamorous Tunisians were in a very different light – and we didn't hear from them again.' As Reiner Moritz said, 'You don't miss that kind of appointment.'

That same evening Kustow attended a farewell dinner for Peter Hall at London's National Theatre and was standing at the pre-dinner drinks when he saw Birkett stride over – straight off the plane from Paris. 'Where is it?' he asked, 'Athens or Tunis?' 'It's Paris.' So the production became French – by default.

Micheline Rozan had, so Birkett said, always secretly wanted Brook to make the film in Paris and specifically at the Bouffes du Nord, which Brook had objected to on the grounds that, 'We wouldn't conceal enough and would soon be seeing the auditorium.' They now had over $3 million but were still some half a million short. Birkett now left his post as executive producer. Propper put down a guarantee for the studios: Joinville was ideal for this kind of international enterprise because there was little union organisation in the studios, while at Boulogne even the builders operated under union laws.

The next and final stage of the story of how the film was ever made covered the frantic weeks of April, May, June and July when virtually the whole of six hours of shooting was organised with the intention of starting in September. Propper had gone into the project with the vaguest idea of what it was all about – 'I just sensed it would be exciting' – so until he went to Glasgow in May 1988 to negotiate the salaries, he had not even seen the production.

Into this hectic period the visit to Japan, in June and July, had to be fitted; also cast changes, thanks to a variety of factors from the availability of actors to the condensing of some roles. The advantage of Paris made itself felt in the number of duplicate French players who could be called in at the last moment. On the other hand they had the daunting task of finding a film crew in a month when thirty films were being shot. The film script also had to be finalised.

In June 1987 Marie-Hélène Estienne and Brook had worked with Carrière on an early draft of the film script which Carrière had arbitrarily cut from the English version as they needed a fake script to impress the Americans. Carrière had, said Brook, 'sat down with a watch and pencil, timed the stage dialogue and put in vague shot directions such as exterior and interior, but no one had time to study it'. So, for virtually the whole preparation period, no one had seen a finished script.

Arjuna's quest for weapons: from an English *Mahabharata* comic

Chloe Obolensky took a two-day break from Tokyo to try and think about the settings. She was desperate to delay the schedule to give herself more time. Propper adamantly refused. She flew from Tokyo to Athens for her break and, to everyone's surprise, returned with a model. There was one black Friday when a deadline for guarantees fell and the missing shortfall reared its ugly head. Channel 4 could supply no money; nor could the BAM. Kustow called this, after the name of his financial director, the 'final Leventhal spasm'. At the last minute a bank was found that was willing to guarantee the money. This averted collapse but, because of the great sum, it was win-all or lose-all at a very personal level.

'Great directors like Bergman,' Brook told me, 'work out every shot; Truffaut knows to the minute the exact length of each film. But when I started working in the theatre my aim was always this: to use as little pre-planned as possible.'

It was well past midnight at the Brasserie Tour d'Argent at the Bastille when Brook finished his account. He talked as volubly and excitedly as when he had begun. 'I'll tell you what I do – and this is temperamental, not a belief. You . . .' – and here he adopted the habit of some religious orders of referring to themselves as another person – 'What matters is that you give yourself freedom. You lay out for yourself the basic ingredients – these pots, and these spices – then, if you improvise, you trust that a result will flow into your hands because you haven't blocked it. The idea is to free the natural forces. So any solution is not quite your own . . . but one you participate in.'

That the filming of *The Mahabharata* should start in Paris in September 1988 seemed an eminently 'Brooktian' solution to all that had happened in the previous six years since 1 September, 1982. Like everything else connected with this epic production, the main complications were closely bound up with Brook's personality. While Kustow had been saying 'Why don't you just bloody well get this movie together?' – and his colleagues could not believe he was still involved with an investment started in 1982 – Brook had simply and slowly been closing ninety-nine of the doors. Each door had been closed behind him, not in front.

As he vividly played each twist and turn of the plot through for me again, I realised that he still remembered just what he had felt like in each of those defeats or trials.

For him, supremely, victory was always a failure, or a series of failures, turned on their head.

7

Ça tourne

With the lamp of word and discrimination one must go beyond word and discrimination and enter upon the path of realisation.

LANKAVATARA SUTRA

*E*veryone in the cast agreed that the filming of *The Mahabharata* came as a final blessing. 'A different rhythm but the same truth,' said Bruce Myers, 'one has to make everything more subtle, more sensitive, more fine in the intimate relationships.' 'The film time is a beautiful time,' commented Urs Bihler. 'In the theatre you carry the whole story and all the scenes before and after – and carry the whole mystery. But on screen in the moment you have just the moment. You have no links' – Miriam Goldschmidt echoed him: 'The film is a healing process.'

But others saw, at least in theory, possible pitfalls. Birkett feared it 'might look like a record of a theatrical production' – on the one hand – and that, conversely, it might go entirely in the dangerous, opposite direction – 'Peter loves the toys of industries . . . it might become over-filmic. Because you can cut, dissolve, pan, it might suddenly become a movie-movie.'

The answer would not lie in trick dissolves, or in electronic wizardry – or in the plains of India – but in translating the real magic on to the screen. As Chloe Obolensky had said, 'We have to change, or decompose the image.'

So the last stage of *The Mahabharata* was reached in September 1988: the wide river was about to join the sea – the sea of faces in a world-wide film and television audience, and to do that it had to broaden its base even more, and certain constituents had to change. 'Faces, places and chases,' someone cracked about the basic needs of the cinema. Would *The Mahabharata* be able to answer them?

Of course, from the beginning it had been a cinematic story: there had always been a network of causes leading to a big event or effect, and there had always been plenty of hidden relationships to discover (or if not discover, speculate upon the nature of their existence). There had also always been a whole series of reversals and other elements of suspense cleverly layered and interrelated. But would the story appear too remote, too much removed from the shaping hands of the characters themselves, or, in other words, too mythical, too unexplained, too riddled with *dei ex machina*?

'We all know the rhythm of dialogue is not the same in a film,' observed Jean-Claude Carrière. 'Dialogue scenes are shorter. The

actors don't have to shout or project. There is much greater freedom – for instance to whisper or to show emotion in close-up. You can isolate someone who looks at someone else. Due to a wheel in the theatre you can imagine Arjuna's chariot from just a wheel. In the film it doesn't work at all. You need more realistic aspects.'

In filming *The Mahabharata* Brook was going to have to realise the quieter, more intimate sides of the characters, heighten their personal moods and conflicts, reveal their weaknesses and strengths, at the sacrifice of the expressive swirl and colour of the theatrical event. Everyone would have to be seen 'living their own turmoil', in Jeffrey Kissoon's phrase.

Joinville Studios, 15 September 1988

The production offices are reached by an iron external staircase outside a disused *plateau* or stage, where the dressing-rooms, make-up rooms and the canteen and other administrative offices and services are also housed. Despite the neat signs in the car-park assigning spaces to the Director, the Director of Photography, and although all the cars are shiny and new – Brook's car a tiny Autobianchi – the rest of the facilities are fairly dilapidated and crumbling: uneven floors in the corridors, cracked wash basins and riven mirrors in the dressing-rooms. Yet *The Mahabharata* company itself, for its fourteen weeks habitation of this shell, is admirably equipped with all the latest technology and comforts.

Some three or four minutes' walk away, on the other side of the compound, stands *Plateau 32, The Mahabharata*'s last home, and its most transformable one, a comfortable, pleasing space electronically modernised in the late 1960s and where, basically, the setting is the same as that in the theatre spaces which preceded it. Still little by way of set, although of course more archways and walls of rock and interior spaces – pillars for palatial openings, rough-cast walls, natural outcrops of rock, rivulets or ponds of water, ground of hardened sand: heat and dust. Myriad formations of wooden and canvased frames covered in polystyrene and coated with sandstone and yellow-ochreous substance, the movable sets can become interiors or exteriors at a few hours' notice, and they are astonishingly adaptable and full of surprises. Nothing has the time to become static.

The visual action of *The Mahabharata* is in the form of a big unfolding or opening out: the first act centres on the game of dice and takes place largely within the suggested confines of palaces or courts; the second is limited by water and forest – with one palace, that of King Virata, concretely invoked; the third is the war, which expands the outside space with plains, cliffs, rivers. The movement is from formality towards freedom.

Willy Lubtchansky with the director

Brook's system of work combines maximum flexibility of imaginative possibility with as little wastage of time as is possible, and to this end he calls rehearsals each day at nine a.m. on the set and gives the lighting designers and the cameramen a chance to work out what is needed, while moving the actors through the necessary positions and running their lines to modify them to the studio auditions, and incorporate any last changes of text or intention. The second hour of the morning is generally taken up with private rehearsals away from the set, while the lights and décors are finally prepared for the shooting. These rehearsals, consisting of finer points of interpretation or personal notes, are conducted by Brook in another studio and room, and generally entail a scaling down of performance, or work on the actors to reveal something particular for the camera. 'We prefer to have the mornings off for rehearsals and practice and costumes,' says Brook.

The third hour of the day, from eleven to twelve, is devoted to ridding the work of the statutory hour of the meal break, by putting it behind one into a position of non-interference. The day proper begins at noon, with the commencement of shooting. The repasts served in the studio canteen are generous, varied and excellent, if sometimes not quite so welcome at eleven a.m. as they might have been later.

Filming has begun slowly as Brook evolves his own method. An assistant tells me that for the birth of the Pandavas (scenes thirty-nine to forty) they had about twenty-three different set-ups and took a day and a half over the scene. At that rate, with two hundred and twenty-five scenes in the script, they will not finish by Easter 1989. The assistant describes Brook's approach as 'flexible' and planned by himself, the Director of Photography, Willy Lubtchansky, and the chief lighting man (Jim Howe). 'You had none of the usual long shot, two-shot close-up technique of American or Australian television. Each shot was beautifully composed.'

I watch a notable sequence, in the first month of filming, some forty-six scenes into the first part, which creates expectation both of the forthcoming game of dice and lays down the hostilities for the subsequent war. It begins with the five Pandavas as young men fighting with the most war-like of the Kauravas, Duryodhana and Dushassana. The as yet unidentified Drona, master of arms, who fights on the Kauravas' side ultimately, arrives at the courtyard and with his combat expertise moves in to separate the assailants.

Then, he goes up to Bhima and takes his wrist; Bhima screams, doubling up with pain. He lets the two brothers go and wants to hit the unknown person who makes some lightning moves. Bhima collapses on the ground. Humiliated, he gets to his feet again.

Above: design detail inside the temple

Right: costumes at Virata's court

Below: (in the set of reeds) special effects
for Ghatotkatcha's plagues

Above: The 'raccord' - adjusting the make-up

Left: night work

Below: studio dichotomy

Rustling up water

Brook on safari

Chloe Obolensky

Below: no man is an island

Above: warming up the need for power

Below: young Karna receiving the magic wand

Gods with actors' fatigue

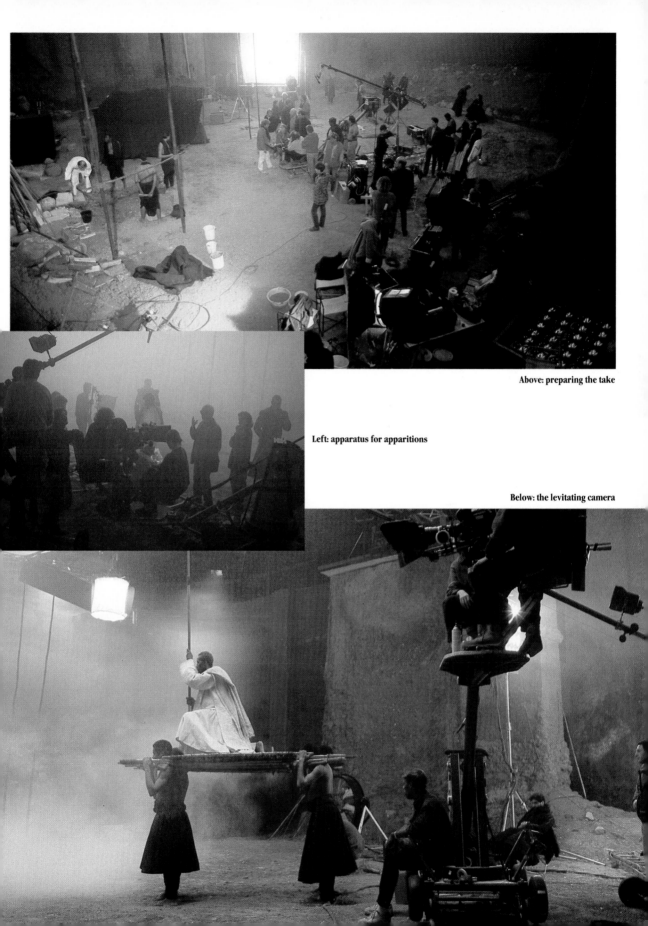

Above: preparing the take

Left: apparatus for apparitions

Below: the levitating camera

Above: second grip in Himalayan snows

Left: plastic refreshment

Below: injured gaffer

Opposite: All aboard the <u>Bhagav</u>

Above: 1st assistant Marc Guilbert

Above: Brook acting referee
with Bhima and Dushassana

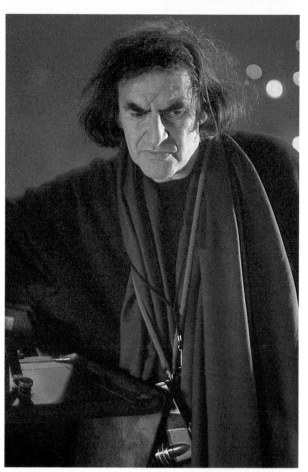

William Lubtchansky

*Then, with a great roar he leaves and comes back immediately
brandishing a tree that he has just pulled out of the ground.*

YUDHISHTHIRA

Bhima! Put down that tree!

BHIMA

No!

ARJUNA

Mind out!

*Everyone moves away except the older man who awaits Bhima
calmly. Just as Bhima tries to hit him with the tree, he moves
away, the tree falls to the ground and Bhima is as though
paralysed, then thrown to the ground by a single flash of the
newcomer's stick. Yudhishthira then asks:*

YUDHISHTHIRA

Who are you?

DRONA

I'm the new teacher.

ARJUNA

What's your name?

YUDHISHTHIRA

Who has sent you?

DRONA

My name is Drona. No one has sent me. I'm here for your
education.

This section, virtually unchanged from the stage version, gives Yoshi Oida the most wonderful opportunity to establish his character's power. Inscrutable, dressed in black, slight of build, and barefoot with a staff – with delicate gestures and a light walk – the Japanese actor could not have shown a stronger contrast to the giant Senegalese Mamadou Dioume who towers over him with a huge knotty piece of tree trunk. Oida has arrived that day with a cold and a stomach bug and others feel threatened, so breaks are filled with discussion of most recently discovered cures for the common cold. In one break, the tall white form and robe of Kouyate's Bhisma completely blots out the monitor-screen.

Brook holds several rehearsals to place the actors. French seems now the predominating first language of his group, so he gives his instructions in French. He wears a dark-blue or black donkey-jacket, pale-blue sweater, jeans and a khaki shirt, and skips round the three powerful men: *'Reste un peu plus près'* . . . *'Tu glisses sur lui . . .'* Expectation builds up and then, at about one p.m. Brook asks for his first take, which is followed by a second and a third; the action explodes magnificently into life, until it is evident that the throwing down of the tree branch creates a problem. Bhima miscalculates and it catches Drona by mistake. It fills the whole monitor-screen. Brook leaves his monitor and goes over to rehearse Mamadou. He tells Oida he is putting in an 'Oh' before each line. Watching the monitor I notice how Lubtchansky is shooting it in an epic style which has a fantastic quality of stillness and very few close-ups. Lubtchansky wears a heavy black corduroy jacket belted with pouches. Invariably, an unlit cigarette dangles from his lips. Huge diffusing screens enclose the unwalled sides of the acting area.

During the next and fourth take Brook's head nods in front of the teacher. Oida achieves a fine blend of radiance and irony: the performance he gives always has two edges, one of comedy, one of high moral intention. 'Cut,' says Brook *'c'est pas mal.'* Someone comes over and whispers to me, 'Brook does not cover himself as a director. He experiments all the time'. Soon the work slows down as they rehearse the next take and the make-up assistants, assistant designer and just about everyone else begin to make these constant physical and practical adjustments which never cease during filming. Inevitably there are breaks in concentration, little pockets of noise, as the momentum of the work rises and falls. *'Encore une répétition pour marquer les places,'* calls Marc, the first assistant.

So it continues all afternoon. No breaks for coffee, no artists' tantrums, no crises, but tough, steady work, with urns of tea and coffee, plates of salami and cheese, well out of sight and sound, for those who need them. The atmosphere is damp and cold, with the sand constantly being sprayed with water to settle it, while 'brick dust' is disseminated from cans to make the air thick and dusty on the screen. Brook comes over during a break in the filming. 'The pace is absolutely horrific,' he says, leaning against the wall: 'One is expected to do high grade work.' His eyes screw up into concentrated pain, 'We've only just begun.'

At five thirty the two groups of cousins now have bows and arrows and they have all moved to a different part of the set which has been elaborately dressed and watered, while tracks and rails and wooden blocks and wedges of every conceivable shape have been laid down for the camera. The work has been intense all afternoon, but only two pages of script have been filmed – and only two scenes. 'It's a return to the early days of filming,' someone says, 'only doing two scenes.' It is the lighting which takes all the time. Jim Howe, the gaffer, strides about purposefully with an astonishing array of tools and gadgets strapped to his waist.

Drona faces a sandstone rampart: 'On top of this wall, I've placed a vulture made of straw and rags. Yudhishthira, take your bow, aim . . .' They do a *mise-en-place*; a set assistant sweeps away the loose stones and covers the boulders with sand; another with a wheelbarrow with sand and pebbles goes around spreading them. Dust rises from the floor. The rival cousins kneel with bows to form a semi-circle facing the film crew and sound boom. '*Silence, on répète,*' calls Marc.

At five forty they are still rehearsing. The actors look tired, although they are used to playing it all night: but ten hours on four pages takes a harder toll. People grow restless, although this is one of the most economic and expressive scenes in the whole play, when Drona asks each cousin what he sees of the vulture and their descriptions belie their skill at archery. Arjuna, who hits the vulture with his arrow, cannot describe it but sees only its eye. This scene is one of many treatments in *The Mahabharata* of the subject of vision, a running form of imagery which underlies a similarity between the epic and *King Lear*. The scene might be subtitled 'How the subjective becomes objective'.

Brook has to deliver a careful telling off, saying he needs complete silence. One senses here a certain conflict between Brook's slow-working improvising methods and the demands of shooting six minutes of film per day. Ten minutes later, as they run the text, the actors fluff their lines. Oida, who has complained earlier of a stomach bug and now looks even more pale, says 'war' instead of 'wall'. Brook takes him and Arjuna aside. To pass the time I make a comparative list of French and English film words with Carole, the continuity girl:

plan serré – close-up
prise – take

feuille de service – call sheet
les rushes – the rushes
l'heure supplémentaire – overtime.

Gilles Abegg, the photographer, is engaged in the most important work of his life. Tall, light-skinned, bespectacled, Abegg mixes inconspicuously with the crew and cast: 'I need,' he says, 'people to make the shot with me.' Since *The Mahabharata* began he has shot some ten thousand colour frames and black and white stills. He still thinks his mission is impossible because Brook dislikes being photographed and having his work photographed: 'The only way is to forget you have a camera and get right to him; your eyes must go through the camera to his.'

Gilles Abegg, with Sergei Obolensky, Draupadi and Krishna *(Photograph by Kim Menzer)*

At six forty-five the plaintive cry still echoes in the *plateau: 'on répète, s'il vous plait!'* And by now the place is full as production staff, accountants, executives and friends have all come down from the offices to watch. The words of the scene have by now been drilled into one's head.

> Drona: What do you see?
> Arjuna: A vulture.
> Drona: Describe the vulture.
> Arjuna: I can't.
> Drona: Why?
> Arjuna: I can only see its eye.
> Drona: Release your arrow.

Filming of this page has become so difficult that wooden wedges have now to be hammered into the floor to mark where the actors kneel. (Sometimes they kneel right on them and wince.) To help the missed arrow shots a red laser-beam is projected on the wall to guide the archers, but the angle of elevation of this goes awry. A Paris pigeon flies in and perches on the red stone buttress, surveying the archery contest. Brook, determined as ever, shuffles back and forth in his blue, hand-knitted sweater. *'Faites le retour comme vous l'avez répété '* he calls sharply, here emanating the sense he likes to drive people hard – particularly towards the end of the day. This becomes the continual pattern; the longer the hours, the harder the work, the more Brook's tenacity and grip tightens. *'On fait les raccords maquillage* (matching up of make-up with previous takes) *et on va tourner,'* he calls.

At seven ten the set is given its final spraying and the familiar dust spreads everywhere to snarl up the actors' throats. *'SILENCE LE ROUGE'*. They begin the take but there is too much dust. The dust eliminators go to work.

'Release your arrows,' completes one take, but Brook feels the tempo had been too slow: he catches every change of pace or nuance. In the last take Mezzogiorno releases the arrow which flies up and sticks in the wall.

Joinville Studios, 18 October, 1988

In the central part of the story, the Pandavas, as a result of the game of dice, are condemned to spend twelve years in exile in the forest, with another year added which they must spend in disguise so they may not be recognised by anyone. Draupadi had been lost to the Kauravas, as Gandhari explained to her husband:

> Draupadi, like all women, made no distinction between her husband and herself. She was part of him, she was him. Whether he lost her before or after, I don't see the difference. Draupadi has been won. I regret to have to say it, but it is so.

But after the failure to strip her naked, because of Krishna's intervention, Draupadi has rejoined her husband. But war, bloody and savage war, is now on the cards. Draupadi swears that war will avenge her.

One of the most spectacular film settings is the court of King Virata, to which the Pandavas repair in exile to spend their appointed year in disguise. Yudhishthira's brothers have already been poisoned by the lake and brought back to life by Yudhishthira's correct answers to the disguised god Dharma.

For the Virata court Brook's idea of improvising his film and its sets, is perhaps most tested. 'It's against all principles of film sets,' he tells me, 'which are built in a permanent architecture on a make or break principle.'

It certainly shows *Plateau 32* at its most versatile; a huge pond covers most of the floor, so a whole subterranean structure has been built beneath the sand. I become struck by the *Tempest*-like quality of this part of the play. Why has Shakespeare's play so possessed Brook's imagination that he seems to reflect it in everything he does? Because it is a God-the-creator's play, an essence of *Genesis*. It asks and answers, if only partially, 'What made the world?' 'Why are we here?'

On one side of the lake are the giant reeds which have been used as the forest; on the other all the technicians. The boom has gone out on a platform when they filmed the lake scene, while the camera has tracked right into the centre of the lake to be close to Bhima and Arjuna dying from the water. Ripples of air have passed across the water, while hours have been spent removing foam bubbles from the surface with butterfly-nets. Obolensky complains about the continual financial compromises affecting filming, now in its seventh week: 'The *roseaux* (reeds) are too tall. I need smaller ones'. The cast are being sprayed from cans to set their hair, or paint their costumes, or moisten their throats: what was life like before the invention of the spray can?

Then, just after the lake sequences have been filmed, the Virata's court rises miraculously in its middle, a platform island of magic, redolent with music and pleasure.

The Pandavas are all in disguise, and Virata's General, Kitchaka, tries to seduce the disguised Draupadi who saves herself by having Bhima take her place in bed. The attempted rape scene proves very difficult, and requires fifteen takes. 'What remains difficult for me,' says Brook yet again, 'what removes pleasure, is the pace of work. Today is a case in point. I have not a clue how to do the Virata court. I see them in the set. The first arrangement doesn't look good. I say, "You do something and I'll look at it . . ." After an hour all these things fall into place. That's why we rehearse.'

But he also draws a great deal on all that has taken place before the filming: he acts, as always, as the collective unconscious memory, as well as the conscious memory, of the whole world of *The Mahabharata*. The Prospero of a subcontinent of words, images and meaning.

Joinville Studios, 9 December 1988

'You say that war is inevitable,' says Arjuna, 'yet you do everything you can to prevent it.'

'Yes,' Krishna replies. 'Everything. That's my role.'

The filming of the war has been prepared weeks before the shooting of it began in November. The word *figuration* in French sounds exotic, but it means merely extras, and the fight extras assemble one Saturday morning with the rest of the cast for a war warm-up in another, bare studio. By now the autumn season of filming has moved into top gear at Joinville, and several other films have joined *The Mahabharata:* one of these became greatly in evidence: a new version of the French Revolution, being filmed for 1989. Outside the rehearsal studio stands a trailer with eleven grey and mud-covered cannon on two levels.

Tent of war in an adjoining studio

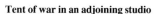

The *figuration* mainly consists of a local karate display group – of somewhat sinister aspect. The fight arranger is the ginger-haired French actor, Alain Maratrat, who played Vyasa in the French version. He arranges everyone in a huge circle and puts them through a complicated repertoire of limbering up, running around and bumping into each other – *'un petit répertoire de petits mouvements de base'*. Toshi Tsuchitori arrives for this rehearsal and provides rhythmic percussion backing. The whole idea is that each time one of the Kauravas meet a Pandava everyone stops and looks.

After some time Brook, who stands to one side of this huge circle like an ageing cherub, clearly delighted, hands in pockets, enjoying the scene – is there any aspect of the production in which he does not participate fully? If so I did not find it – Brook intercedes, and in French re-organises the circle so that now some people form an inner circle, some an outer. I think of T. S. Eliot's line

I see crowds of people, walking round in a ring.

He then instructs Joseph Kurian, the Indian martial arts specialist from Kerala, to show some forms of attack and defence to certain of the fighters, and, while they kick and lash out, he stands back, involved with and feeding off this huge display of energy from all the various groups.

What the actors give out is his food, and, gourmet and gourmand at the same time, here is a feast to be enjoyed, as well as directed. He calls out instructions, *'Essayez de faire parfaitement ensemble . . . beaucoup plus rapprochés, plus serrés'* . . . He tells the assistants, Marc and Philippe, to photograph certain effects, as for instance when he draws up everyone in two long battle-lines. The lines then have to move forward two feet at a time.

For the filming of the war Brook and Obolensky have to concentrate the space even more than in other parts of the film, and present and select aspects of it. They can rely less on making the action penetrate the viewer, and being able to involve him totally. Inevitably it becomes more of a spectacle, an arrangement of aspects of the fighting, and to this extent depersonalised in relation to the play. One extremely significant difference is the use of fighting men: in the play the generals do all their own fighting and now this has to be delegated to the extras; another is the necessary expansion of physical resources – shields, fighting-weapons, chariots, horses.

The two main weapons, in the attempt to universalise the war, remain light and smoke. The strong, unearthly apocalyptic light is achieved by what Jim Howe calls 'a twenty-five kilowatt projector for a unique sunlight effect.' He explains how difficult the war scenes are: they are a climax to all the difficulties of filming *The*

Mahabharata. 'Very complicated in a small space with a lot of actor movement. To begin with I've used high-key, side lighting, high-key back lighting, but Brook, by the end, did not want to see the walls. As in a laboratory we've discovered everything ourselves.'

A basic element is giving the film what Howe calls different 'colour temperature'. In the same décors they have to create the effects of different times of day or night – e.g. very low light-angles for sunrise. Brook increasingly evolves a taste for the mysterious gloom. 'He didn't want a rich lighting to "break" people out. He wanted it to look gloomy, to give dimension to the gloom. To use the space, light it, and then side light or back light it with soft reflection for contour.'

Howe is not at all in favour of stereotype cinema images, and finds working with Brook and Lubtchansky fascinating, as they constantly 're-evolved the same space'. The results never fall into cliché: he feels it is a fantastic work-experience, although 'a lot of people wouldn't have worked so hard'. Brook trusts people, never puts them in question, and he approves of Brook's 'very stable and constant speed of working. Usually after three months of shooting it slows down. But not with Brook, he calibrates at a certain speed and has a way of keeping things up.'

Smoke? 'There is never enough and I'm frightened of having too much,' says Willy Lubtchansky as we survey the pall which hangs over the battlefield of cliffs and rocky surfaces for the death of Bhima. Lubtchansky, like Brook, underlines the problems of time and its effect on the quality of work. The continuity, generally, is a headache, for sometimes it takes a week to get the lighting right – sometimes it has to be stylised, sometimes natural.

A man hoses the battlefield before Dushassana, in a protracted and bloodthirsty scene, almost disposes of the giant Pandava. Dioumé has mud all over his hair and has pricked his chest to produce blood. Bihler, as Dushassana, pursues him with an axe, but suddenly Bhima turns the fight, pulls his opponent over by the ankle, overcomes him and finally rips open his belly, drinks his blood and eats his entrails. This is what he had vowed to do when Dushassana insulted Draupadi. The boy is watching all this. 'We weren't born to be happy,' says Bhima as he walks out of frame. The camera creates a wonderful fluency and juxtaposition of shapes on the screen.

There had been some problem on the set half an hour before over make-up and costume, and tempers have been frayed. Pippa Cleator comes up and remarks, 'Very interesting, filming, it's a study in problem solving. Every hour something appalling comes up, but everyone is under such pressure that you can't form grudges or find the anger to continue with people afterwards. You have to resolve everything in the moment.'

A film is made three times. First in the pre-production work of the writers and the director – and, in the case of *The Mahabharata*, in the years of improvisations, study, and the performances by the cast. Second, there is the actual shooting, in the case of *The Mahabharata*, a process as improvised and unexpected as much of the early preparatory work itself. Third, there is the editing, which is a creative reinterpretation, or indeed a re-making, of all that has been assembled; in the case of *The Mahabharata* some 700 cans, containing 100,000 feet of film, stacked in neatly carpentered shelves in the

Nicolas Gaster

139

processing plant at Joinville. Of course editing, in the juxtaposition of
the images, in its selection and arrangement, can be extremely
influential and even change the course and direction of sequences,
alter the mood, and bring a completely new and utterly unexpected
dimension to the filmed work.

Brook is very specific as to what he requires from his editor.
'French directors,' he tells me, 'recognise the artistic importance of
the cameraman and hardly any director feels he works his own
camera. But a director stands over the editor and, as a result, there
are not such good editors in France. Now in the Anglo-American
tradition, the editor is as equally respected as the cameraman and
brings his own very special contribution.'

This was why he opted for the English editor, Nick Gaster,
underlining also the importance that the editor's language be the
same as the film's dialogue.

Gaster is uncompromising about his own importance in re-making
The Mahabharata, which he calls 'a huge novel'. 'Editing is a great
power trip. All kinds of subtle things happen,' he says, 'like you find
a situation where a whole battle scene can be better replaced by a line
of dialogue, or a whole page of dialogue replaced by a look. You
have to give up your most cherished moments.'

One cannot help also feeling that Gaster worships at the
fountain-head of Brook's inspiration; for when he talks of the magical
quality of some of Krishna's long speeches, which had been played in
one shot, he extols the existential quality of cinema, and how
something indefinable happens between the audience and the work:
'After the first cut it is a constantly evolving process, you get the
opportunity to change the rhythm, to juxtapose or change order of
scenes and increase or decrease dramatic tension.'

Every day of shooting takes two or three days of editing by
Gaster and his three associates. Gaster expresses concern about how
the studio circumstances have tended to quieten down the actors, also
to slow them down. 'I have to speed them up. It's a very classical
studio film. And I was worried at the beginning about the exterior
sets. But when you see it as a piece the stronger parts lift the weaker
pieces. I thought it was going to be the other way round.'

The Mahabharata is Gaster's biggest ever assignment and being
'Marxist-orientated' he is not very interested in the religion. 'The
editor must always be one step ahead, never two. He is the invisible
guide – if the audience is confused, then he has gone too far ahead. If
you see the editing, then you've failed. It's like the engine of a car,
you don't see it, but it keeps everything moving. It is the fundamental
creator of tension, because of the transitions between scenes and
between characters. Half the interest of any conversation is on the
person who is not talking. It's much more manipulative than the

theatre, and you have to use the imagination of your audience. Brook breaks down everyone's habits, including mine.'

One lunchtime, near the half-way mark, at what must have seemed to him the lowest point in the filming, Brook comes over to the table in the studio canteen where I am seated and sits down opposite me. He complains of the pressure of work. He appears, unusually for him, very drained: his skin is pale, his light blue eyes sapped of colour and deeply hidden beneath his brows – as if dazzled by the sun – his head sunk in an almost Churchillian heaviness between his shoulders. Unusually for him, too, he eats the whole lunch that is set before him.

But he soon begins to talk, astonishingly enough – trying, perhaps at first, to force himself out of the fatigue – and energy returns as he begins expanding on two themes, one well known, the other a complete surprise. The first is that Shakespeare is the greatest expression of the spirit of the English, whom he affectionately calls the 'most poetical, mystical people on earth'.

In contrast to his enthusiasm for Shakespeare, he is firm in his dislike for most drama being written in England at the moment, which treats life 'merely as a humanist problem' – the best that the critics ever say about a new play is that it is 'Shavian, intelligent, sceptical'.

The second of his themes makes me sit up even more. After asserting – quite apart from any assent or encouragement from me – his belief in specifically religious burial services, and condemning humanist and present-day Russian practices – 'where there are only the flowers, the speeches and a bit of Tchaikovsky' – he goes on that only when he came to Glasgow with *The Mahabharata* did he realise for the first time since 'I'd deserted England and gone my own way', how 'profoundly English' it is. 'Behind all the façade, with a French text, with all these different elements, peoples and cultures, *The Mahabharata* is in that same romantic, mystical tradition as Shakespeare, and the essence of both remains their spiritual power.' After all the talk of universality we are back to W. B. Yeats's 'two eternities' of race and soul.

With this perception of Brook's – and perhaps only a shifting and temporary one – the other, enduring strand of the work of the theatre magician must finally be emphasised. The ritualisation of action – with which Brook had begun with Vivien Leigh in *Titus Andronicus* – and in particular the echoing images, have become multiplied a hundred-fold by the time of *The Mahabharata*. But the magic remains the same, based on a simple perception of what will best bring something to life.

When the Princess Draupadi, paragon of women, joint wife of the Pandavas, is lost by Yudhishthira to his mortal foe Duryodhana in the game of dice, she is commanded to strip so that the Kauravas can see her naked. Here the prodigy of protection given to her by the god, Krishna, who will not allow her enemies to be gratified, is shown by the use of a simple long scarf which Dushassana pulls and pulls, to symbolise the endless layers of cloth the god provides. The power of magic and spiritual protection is unlimited, that of human will strictly curtailed.

8

How does he have such energy?

Je suis le champ vil des sublimes combats.
VICTOR HUGO

'*B*eginnings are often secret,' says Vyasa. 'So are endings, so is process,' added a Los Angeles journalist who sought out Brook during the early part of filming at Joinville. Her name was Joyce Reed, and she descended on Brook one lunchtime.

'I want to put to you a personal question – off the record and just for my own private interest . . .' Brook looked at the miniature tape recorder she had taken from her bag and had placed beside her fork, on the table. He said to me, in an aside, 'People have these tapes on the table like mineral water'.

Her finger flicked the tape on, although she had offered not to, as Brook, not too emphatically, had said, 'Please don't . . .'

'You look so wonderful, so calm . . .' asserted the journalist.

Brook perked up. 'It's always wonderful when people say that to me. It's so much better than saying how awful you look. I'm like a film actor to whom if you say, "look tired" I look tired. I am like that. If you tell me I look good, I look good.'

Ms Reed, a kindly looking lady, a Brook fanatic who had come all the way just from L.A. popped in her leading question – she was astute enough to know she was only going to have time for one.

'How do you have such energy? What is your secret?' There was a pause. 'How do you always look so composed? Do you practise yoga or meditation?'

I squirmed slightly, aware this was causing Brook embarrassment. He looked and smiled at me and then said nothing.

Nothing went on for some time. Someone else came to the table and asked Brook a question. After a while the defeated journalist brought out a copy of Brook's second book, *The Shifting Point*, published in 1988, and asked him to sign it. He took a pen and wrote swiftly on the prelim blank page, and then pushed the copy over to Ms Reed.

'I will answer with a riddle,' he had written. 'Why does Hamlet say, "As swift as meditation?"'

Ms Reed was deeply gratified. There was a brief discussion. Brook said, 'There is nothing as swift as simultaneity – it is an absolute, faster than light. When people think of meditation they think of slow, painful thought, of passivity – there is no reason why thought should not be positive and swift.'

Brook was then interrupted by the sound technician and Ms Reed, in an extended aside to me, praised Brook's influence on her, telling me how he 'freed' her and helped her to uncover blocks inside her personality.

Brook turned back to her. She fished out a technical question she had written on a card – about whether he had changed his technique for the filming of *The Mahabharata*. He answered:

'I never work with a pre-conceived plan. It is not like a woman who conceives a baby, and you know what is coming, and you plan for it. I am more like a sculptor who has a block of stone. I do not know what is going to emerge. I have a dimly glimpsed idea of some possibility . . . I see its chance to emerge, but I want to wait. I don't like to say anything about it. Now we have the stage production behind us, I can talk about that, but I cannot talk about the film until it is over. You'll have to ask me later.'

End of interview. I never tried out these particular questions on Brook. But I did ask most of the others I talked to:

'How does he have such energy?'

Marie-Hélène Estienne replied, almost without thinking, 'Oh that's easy. He does not lose it!' When I frowned with incomprehension she went on, 'He does not get angry. He's very observant. Everyone loves him. He knows what he wants.' And so on. More significantly, 'He finds a way without formulating it.' She added in French that he was, '*conscient, pas intellectuel*', and that, 'You could help him by going with him'.

All this was fairly elliptical. It was a bit like the time when I asked a leading member of the cast what Brook said at his private note sessions. He never berates you, I was told, and years later you could never remember what had been said. It had gone into you, become part of you and been forgotten.

Bob Lloyd, when questioned about Brook's energy, just regretted that the speech he most liked in the whole play had had to be cut from the film:

> I am all that is not yet here, all that is still to come, I am the
> ancestor, I am space, the cause of any birth is myself, I am the
> limit of everything, tireless, indestructible.

This was from the part of the Wise Man. Could this explain Brook's energy?

Reiner Moritz believed the answer lay in Brook's asceticism. 'If he said he's entering a Zen monastery I'd believe him . . . He's very careful in preparing things and has a wonderful way of seeing turns of hand. Always calm and on top of situations.' Birkett said, 'He's a universal spirit.' But William Wilkinson believed, on a more technical level, that much of his energy stemmed from attending rehearsals: after a long and tiring day of organising he had seen him go off to rehearse and emerge again later fresh and full of energy.

Kustow asserted that Brook's constant power of recharging himself found its source in his sense of danger – as he is a man who is constantly walking a tight-rope. He does not believe in a basic order, or that any single phenomenon is definitive. 'He regards it, by second nature, as part of a web of other events that are going to happen. He never loses sight of the web or his place in it, knowing what looks like a disaster can, given time and a few different twists, become a victory.'

Now sixty-four, Brook has a tougher and more grizzled air which would seem to belie completely that earlier impression of gilded and cosseted youth described by Tynan. But is this appearance not equally a mask and an enigma? 'One sees that the usual facial expression,' he writes in his brilliant essay about masks, 'either conceals that it's not in tune with what is really going on inside (so it's a mask in that sense), or it is a decorated account.' For some people, for example Diana Rigg, it is the stillness which is the most striking thing about him: 'Peter's Svengali effect.' For the critic Bernard Levin his face is never in repose, but anxiously seeking new horizons.

'The only part I would be right for is Hamlet,' Brook had once said. But this was at the time when success was making him more dictatorial in his methods, and when one member of his cast of *Romeo and Juliet* complained of high-handedness, and of being master-minded, through the ball and fight scenes, by means of a megaphone. Yet behind the martinet manner the personal voice soon became audible: so that as far back as 1961 Brook was able to state with authority – and he had not yet reached forty – 'I want to see a flood of people and events that echo my inner battlefield. I want to see behind this desperate and ravishing confusion an order, a structure that will relate to my deepest and truest longings for structure and law.'

Freddie Jones, acting in *U.S.* once said, 'Three people I can't get a bead on: a madman, a drunk, and Peter!' The great paradox that Brook presents today is that he can apparently embrace and embody complete opposites in a totally relaxed and assured way. It is as if, sometimes, when appearing to be playing his biggest hoax, he reveals his truest feeling. Paul Scofield has described him as able 'to be at once open and closed. Open to a multitude of influences, like a water-creature taking invisible nourishment from the sea – while at the same moment his eyes are fixed on the final objective and closed to anything irrelevant to its demands'.

Most people, at some time or other, seem to trap themselves, or

become trapped by circumstances. Not Brook. His options are always open. He somehow manages never to put himself in the kind of double-bind from which escape is difficult. Instead, a multiple orientation of view brings him security. The key to this, perhaps, is that he never believes one thing is specifically better – or more true – than another. The title *The Shifting Point* confirms this ambiguity. He says in the preface:

> I have never believed in a single truth. Neither my own, nor those of others. I believe all schools, all theories can be useful in some place, at some time. But I have discovered that one can only live by a passionate, and absolute, identification with a point of view.

We should not take this too seriously. Birkett describes how Brook likes to set his friends Zen riddles: 'There is a bird in a cage,' Brook told him one day – and then with great technical precision described the cage. 'It had bars an inch apart – it was seamlessly made of wood and was two inches across at its narrow end. How could it escape?'

Birkett pondered the problem, brows knit, considering all the logistical and structural possibilities, but could not see a single way through the difficulties. Then for some seconds Brook looked at him. He clapped his hands lightly, his eyes lit up – 'It's free,' he declared.

At the end of *U.S.* Brook played a trick on the audience which also became one of his master images: the burning of the butterfly. Bob Lloyd entered with a small table which had a little black box standing on it. Opening the box, he released several white butterflies, which fluttered off. He then pulled out a lighter from his pocket, ignited it and taking from the box another white butterfly held it up to the flame and burnt it.

When they were working this out, Brook told the stage manager, 'I am not going to require any actor to burn a butterfly,' so they devised a twist of silver paper which they impregnated with sulphur. Brook further admonished the stage manager, 'You are to tell nobody in the world that we are *not* burning a butterfly.'

The trick succeeded in so far as audiences believed butterflies were being burned. After several nights of *U.S.* an RSPCA inspector called at the Aldwych stage door to discuss the issue with the stage manager, and became very threatening in his determination to stop the burning, whereupon the stage manager panicked and told him, 'I'm not supposed to tell you this, but it's not a real butterfly.' At this juncture Brook suddenly appeared behind the stage manager.

He addressed the officer from the RSPCA. 'This is not your

lucky day,' he told him. 'This man (he indicated the stage manager) is not supposed to have told you this. If you inform your membership we are not burning the butterfly, from that day forward we will *start* to burn the butterfly!'

I never worked directly with Brook at Stratford. I heard that he responded favourably to a production I did in the Stratford Studio of Ben Jonson's *Catiline* with Roy Dotrice and Janet Suzman, pretentiously performed in a somewhat Artaudesque manner. (This was just before the *Theatre of Cruelty* season at LAMDA, and when this kind of experiment was very much in the air.) At Stratford, where I assisted on a poor but happy *Julius Caesar*, I did hear about an ill-fated production of *The Tempest*, on which Brook worked with Clifford Williams as his assistant. Rehearsals started badly with the summary sacking of Caroline Hunt, daughter of Hugh Hunt, who had been cast as Miranda. But the design caused the worst problems of all. Abd'Elkader Farrah's set had been cleverly conceived as a Perspex shell, which, according to the way it was lit, could be opaque one minute and transparent the next. This complicated idea was further entangled with a series of traps cut in the false floor and a 'travelator' designed to convey characters across the proscenium. Four diminutive actors doubled Ian Holm, who played Ariel.

Rehearsals became a nightmare. According to one member of the cast:

> More than once Miranda was reduced to tears and very experienced actors would cringe in fear of Brook's cutting tongue. The three Goddesses were played by Susan Engel, Cherry Morris and Janet Suzman making her début with the RSC. They were to appear as giantesses wearing twelve-foot high puppets on cane frames like corn dollies. However the frames proved too heavy for them and they could neither see nor be heard from inside the costume.

After the dress rehearsal Brook gave a scathing note session, taking the cast apart one by one and making personal remarks aimed at their most vulnerable spot, so that the group was reduced to a group of resentful, miserable individuals united in their hatred of the director. The actors realised later that this was exactly Brook's intention: knowing the production was doomed, he saw that its only hope lay in the actors pulling it together, and in their having a common bond of hatred in order to do that. In fact it became, ultimately, a happy show.

Brook is universally believed to have the infallible touch: I relate this account of failure to give another dimension to the man. Brook *can* be angry, he can behave ungraciously, rudely and furiously, and usually when he does so, it is in the context of his family of actors. Rehearsals are where he relaxes and recharges his batteries, which is why, perhaps, once he began his full dedication to experiment, the range of actors and actresses with whom he can work has become more limited (and more limited, specifically, with regard to English women: there are none in *The Mahabharata*). Brook is frank that he enjoys the theatre, having stated in *The Empty Space*, 'I have the greatest respect for other people's pleasure, and particularly for anyone's frivolity. I came to the theatre myself for sensual and often irresponsible reasons. Entertainment is fine.'

I was struck at once, when I met Brook again, by the degree to which, at least in appearance and manner, he had mellowed. The hair had now become very white, the features were perhaps larger and more fleshy, giving an impression more of dignity than of intellectual sharpness. Wearing a pale green sweater beneath a white jacket with greenish, canvas trousers – and with his very mobile features and eagerness of response – there was something particularly gentle and unassuming about his manner. Gone was that power to transfix the young, upwardly aspiring director. The seething turmoil I used to feel in the presence of the 'Great Man' subsided in an instant. When I later compared my impression with Bob Lloyd, he confirmed that Brook had, with the passing of years, become more sociable and warm: 'That makes it seem he wasn't years ago,' Lloyd said. Lloyd confessed that he also used to be terrified of Brook, and always felt you had to be so certain in front of him, when he looked at you with 'Gurdjieff's eyes', that it was much more easy to walk out in front of an audience with lights than perform under his gaze. He quoted four lines from Ezra Pound as being particularly relevant to his feeling about Brook:

Go my songs and seek your praise from the
Young and intolerant
Seek ever to stand in the hard Sophoclean light
And take your wounds from it gladly.

But, of course, Brook had not become entirely modest. As he once pointed out, 'It is the modest director, the honourable unassuming one, often the nicest man, who should be trusted least.' We must remember that when he was seven he directed his own first theatre production in front of his parents, acting every part himself. The notebook he retained was inscribed '*Hamlet* by P. Brook and W. Shakespeare'.

Brook has gone on developing all his life: increasingly, he claims less and less authority over what happens in his productions. Scofield's judgment of the change is again impeccable:

> He relies more and more on his own nature, and less and less on
> his intellectual judgment which is considerable . . . He has
> shifted from spectatorship to participation, from remote control
> to a more sensual involvement. I think he would like the
> experience of being a director to be closer to that of the
> performer.

Michael Kustow, on the other hand, has described how, in the repeated expositions that Brook did in order to raise money for the filming of *The Mahabharata*, he behaved as if it were a kind of performance – 'Not a show-off, but a reiteration tested anew each time for the truth and freshness . . . as he sits there with his hands clasped, his upper body motionless, his pale blue eyes sweeping the table, there doesn't seem to be any division between the way he makes his theatre and the way he lives his life.'

In the past he could play many parts: according to the writer John Heilpern, 'the hard director, the friendly father figure, the earnest student, secret confidant, manipulator, analyst, guide . . . ' His nicknames reveal quite a bit about him: 'The Guru', 'The Ogre', 'The Monster', 'The Buddha', 'The Gnome', 'King of the Trolls'. When Heilpern first met Brook he asked him what he saw as his greatest fault, and after a long, agonised silence, during which Brook stared intensely into the distance, he replied 'What *is* a fault?'

Today his reticence seems to be raising fewer protective barriers. He began to see indecisiveness might be a virtue during rehearsals of *A Midsummer Night's Dream*. The actor John Kane wrote of the rehearsals:

> Peter takes so long over the occasional word that you begin to
> suspect he may have a speech impediment. He looks at the
> ceiling or at the floor. His hands become soft-pink pincers
> moulding ideas like pie-crust. He pokes his head forward as if to
> propel his thought across the distance that separates us. In the

silences, we sift his unfinished sentences in our minds, trying to supply the missing magic word that will transform our dullness and re-establish communication.

Perhaps leaving England enabled Brook, finally, to stop playing the many-sided, defensive role of the director: 'No man is a prophet in his own country'. France allowed him his full stature. As Birkett says, 'He gets more and more what he is'. Reiner Moritz describes him as 'shining from within', and as 'one of the few people who has reached a degree of serenity due to insight'. Bruce Myers claims that Brook, like all of us, has had to go through stages. 'You have to go through wildness. You go through things which at a professional level are the same as at a personal level.'

Over twenty years ago Brook described his own inner realism as a state of flux – that it could only be understood with a flash of recognition 'that tells me it is true, because it is also in me'. A careful look at that enigmatic face confirms he is in touch with the sufferings of this world – inside himself and in others and that, like the poet Keats, he will not let them rest.

Brook has, since the commencement of *The Mahabharata* project, formed a close working relationship with Marie-Hélène Estienne, whom he had first met when she worked as a journalist on *Les Nouvelles Littéraires*. He had said to her, she recalled, 'Why write about things, why not do them?' and he started her off by asking her to cast *Timon of Athens* in 1974. On *The Mahabharata* she became much more than Brook's assistant. A prodigious worker she has operated as co-ordinating genius, intimately in touch with all

sides of the production. Her memory, grasp of detail, and range of critical and intuitive response have all been phenomenal. In recognition of this Brook dedicated the published English version of *The Mahabharata* 'To Marie-Hélène Estienne, who has held the threads of *The Mahabharata* together through two languages, four continents, eight years.'

Brook's sense of caution is underlined by a story Birkett tells of a play he has never attempted. Birkett was listening to *La Forza del destino* in his car one day and Brook said to him 'Oh you must turn that down. Don't you know it's notoriously unlucky, like *Macbeth*?' Birkett enquired what it was about the *Macbeth* story that made the reaction of this most rational man so strong, and ventured to ask why he had never directed the play. '*Macbeth* is a disaster play,' Brook told him: 'Shakespeare just looked too far into things he shouldn't have.' Yet I wonder if it is not the fact that Macbeth is prey throughout to a very Christian, almost sentimental, form of conscience that has alienated Brook from this play. This gives Macbeth sympathy, and cannot be stripped away without destroying the core of the play.

Others stress how Brook is always ready to work, and how he will never push actors into areas where he is not prepared to go himself: Mireille Maalouf records, 'Peter is always working – we are all contaminated with the virus of work', while Pippa Cleator calls him, 'the filter through which everything passes'.

I conclude that the prime source of Brook's energy comes from his ability to allow a process to work itself out in the belief that everything of life is part of some larger design – of which we can only, however perceptive we are, dimly perceive the plan.

To achieve this you have to be 'in touch' – with yourself and with others – and to be open and available to what others are feeling and thinking. Then to pick up and use the best of it.

I was constantly impressed how Brook, apart from rehearsing and filming *The Mahabharata*, with all the myriad detail and grinding pressure this involved, always greeted each new arrival in the studio with individual and curious attention, eager for a new face, a new vibration of response. Of course, all through filming, there is always an audience. But Brook seemed nevertheless to have an insatiable lust for finding out about people. He continually registered who you were and what you were saying to him. Perhaps he wishes to extend the self-knowledge he has attained indefinitely, so that others may also benefit from this gift. As Mezzogiorno says, 'Peter is more clear, he sees better. When you speak with him you feel that he sees you clearly. He is like a person who doesn't drink among drunk people.'

With *The Mahabharata*, Brook, by dint of long obedience to discipline and hard work, has achieved a work of unforced spontaneity and consummate art. There is much of the 'negative capability' of Keats in this achievement: long sympathy with spiritual disciplines and religious feeling has brought him to a position neither of rigid stoicism nor of mere passivity, but to one of active resignation. The work exemplifies the perfect marriage of the religious temperament and artistic dedication as expressed by Huxley in *The Perennial Philosophy*:

> Knowing that he can never create anything on his own account, out of the top layers, so to speak, of his personal consciousness, he submits obediently to the workings of 'inspiration'; and knowing that the medium in which he works has its own self-nature, which must not be ignored or violently overridden, he makes himself its patient servant.

CAST AND PRODUCTION CREDITS

(in alphabetical order)

Erika Alexander	Madri / Hidimbi
Maurice Benichou	Kitchaka
Amba Bihler	Virata's daughter
Lou Bihler	young Karna
Urs Bihler	Dushassana
Ryszard Cieslak	Dhritharashtra
Georges Corraface	Duryodhana
Jean-Paul Denizon	Nakula
Mamadou Dioume	Bhima
Miriam Goldschmidt	Kunti
Hapsari Hardjito	Abhimanyu's wife
Nolan Hemmings	Abhimanyu
Ken Higelin	deathless boy
Ciaran Hinds	Aswatthaman
Gisèle Hogard	1st princess
Corinne Jaber	Amba / Sikhandin
Lutfi Jakfar	Uttara
Akram Khan	Ekalavya
Jeffrey Kissoon	Karna
Sotigui Kouyate	Bhisma
Joseph Kurian	Drishtadyumna
Tuncel Kurtiz	Shakuni
Robert Langdon Lloyd	Vyasa
Clement Masdongar	Gazelle
Leela Mayor	Satyavati
Vittorio Mezzorgiorno	Arjuna
Bruce Myers	Ganesha / Krishna
Yumi Nara	Virata's wife
Tamsir Niane	Urvasi
Yoshi Oida	Drona
Hélène Patarot	Gandhari
Abbi Patrix	Salva
Julie Romanus	2nd princess
Bakary Sangare	the Sun / Rakshasa / Ghatotkacha
Mallika Sarabhai	Draupadi
Andrzej Seweryn	Yudhishthira

Mas Soegeng	Virata
Antonin Stahly-Vishwanadan	the boy
Tapa Sudana	Pandu / Shiva / Salya
Mahmoud Tabrizi-Zadeh	Sahadeva
Myriam Tadesse	Gandhari's servant
Velu Vishwanadan	the hermit
Directed by	Peter Brook
Produced by	Michel Propper
Screenplay by	Peter Brook
	Jean-Claude Carrière
	Marie-Hélène Estienne
Director of photography	William Lubtchansky
Production designer	Chloe Obolensky
1st assistant director	Marc Guilbert
2nd assistants	Philippe Tourret
	Josef Baar
Editor	Nicolas Gaster
Sound	Daniel Brisseau
	Dominique Dalmasso
Production supervisor	Christine Raspillère
Executive producers	Michael Birkett
	Harvey Lichtenstein
	Michael Kustow
Co-producers	Edward Myerson
	Micheline Rozan
	Rachel Tabori
	William Wilkinson
Continuity	Carole Fèvre
Music by	Toshi Tsuchitori
	Djamchid Chemirani
	Kudsi Erguner
	Kim Menzer
	Mahmoud Tabrizi-Zadeh
Songs interpreted by	Sarmila Roy
Music produced by	Philippe Eidel

ACKNOWLEDGMENTS

As this is my seventh or eighth book for the same publisher I would particularly like to thank Hodder & Stoughton as a whole, as well as those especially concerned with its production. I thank Simone Mauger, for enthusiastically overseeing all aspects of the text's editing and layout; and Henry Steadman for his responsive design. I must also express my warmest gratitude to Ion Trewin, Editorial Director at Hodders, for a rich and close collaboration which began with *Ralph Richardson: An Actor's Life*, first published in 1982.

I would also like to thank Reiner Moritz for his generous support, and Sally Fairhead, of RM Associates, for her unflagging zeal in the cause of this book, and her resourceful supply of material and information.

Finally I, the publisher and RM Associates give our thanks to the following organisation and individuals for their co-operation in making this book possible: all the artists and personnel involved with the filming of *The Mahabharata*; CICT; the producers and copyright holders in the television production, Channel Four Television, the Brooklyn Academy of Music, Mahabharata Ltd and Les Productions du 3ème Etage, the associate producers Danmarks radio, SVT1, RTVE, NOS-TV, La SEPT, Channel 3 Finland, BRT, Channel 2 Iceland, NRK, RTP, SBS TV, ORF, BR/WDR, Pioneer LDC, Inc and Doordarshan TV; Gilles Abegg, Sygma, Sergei Obolensky, Alan Wylie and Guido Mangold for permission to reproduce photographs; The British Library for permission to reproduce illustrations from the *Bhagavad Gita*; Rhys McConnochie for permission to quote from his article 'Even Peter Brook has Flops', published in Australia in 1988; and Amar Chitra Katha for reproduction of the cartoon from the English comic of The Mahabharata, published by India Book House.

Index

Figures in italics refer to captions.

TM = The Mahabharata

157

158

Mnouchkine, Ariane, 40, 69
Moderato Cantabile, 29
Monde, Le, 61
Moritz, Reiner, 115, *115*, 116, 122, 144, 151
Morley, Robert, 33
Morris, Cherry, 148
Munshi, K. M., 96
Musée de L'Homme, Paris, 104
music, 108–10
Myers, Bruce, 72, 84–5, 125, 151

Nahusha, 4
Nakamura, Hitomi, 79–80
Nakula, 3, 4, 5, 76
National Endowment for the Arts, 118
National Theatre (London), 122
Nehru, Jawaharlal, 114
Nepal, 109
New Delhi, 103
New York, 55, 70, 72, 73, 94, 112, 117
New York Times, 70, 72
New Yorker, 72
Niane, Tamsir, 92
Noh theatre, 93
Nomura, Takashi, 80
Nouvelles Littéraires, Les, 151

Oakley, Barry, 74
Obolensky, Chloe, 123, 125, 135
    and Majestic Theater, New York, 70, 106
    and Old Transport Museum, Glasgow, 76, 107
    Ratcliffe reviews costumes, 78
    Brook on, 100
    visits India, 101, 102, 103
    and the Bouffes, 102, 103
    costume research, 104
    collaboration with Brook, 104
    and open-air venues, 106–7
    and film, 107–8
    and filming of the war in *TM*, 137
Obolensky, Sergei, *132*
Observer, 65, 78
Oedipus (Seneca), 39
Oida, Yoshi, 40, 80, 81–2, 93, 109, 130
Okura, 93
Old Transport Museum, Glasgow, 76, 103, 107, 119
Old Vic, 39
Olivier, Laurence (Baron Olivier of Brighton), 33
Oooka, Makoto, 79
Open Theatre, 39, 42
Orghast at Persepolis, 43
Orion, 112
Oxford University Film Society, 30

Pandavas, 3–10, 22, 59, 81, 84, 87, 88, 90, 128, 134, 135, 137, 139, 141
Pandu, 2–3, 4, 5, 6
Paris, 122
Parry, Natasha, 33–4
Pasupata (the supreme weapon), 7
Patarot, Hélène, *89*
Peaslee, Richard, 109
Perennial Philosophy, The (Huxley), 58, 153
Perth, Australia, 73, 74, 75, 92, 103, 106, 107
Perth Advertiser, 74
Perth Festival, 111
Peter, John, 61, 79
Picker, David, 113
Planchon, Roger, 111
Plateau 32, 20, 127, 134
Poland, 111
Polanski, Roman, 120
Pound, Ezra, 149
Power and the Glory, The (Greene), 33
Prabhupada, Swami, 48
Propper, Michel, 122, 123

props, 100, 104, 106
Puru, 4
Puttnam, David, 113

Racine, Jean, 49, 51
Rakshasha, 7
Raleigh Studio Theatre, 69, 106
Ramayana, The, 60
Ratcliffe, Michael, 65–6, 70, 78
Real Thing, The (Stoppard), 49
Reed, Joyce, 143, 144
Renaud, Madeleine, 49
Return of Martin Guerre, The (Vigne), 49
Rich, Frank, 70–1, 72
Rigg, Diana, 145
Ring Round the Moon (Anouilh), 32
Rishi Atri, 4
Rishni, 4
RM Associates, 115, 116
Rockefeller Foundation, 111, 117
Rolling Stone, 49
Romeo and Juliet (Shakespeare), 145
Roundhouse, 39, 118
Roussin André, 33
Royal Shakespeare Company, 27, 38, 69, 148
Rozan, Micheline, 38, 43, 47, 116, 118, 122, 123
RSPCA (Royal Society for the Prevention of Cruelty to Animals), 147
R.T.F., 112
Russian Empire: a Portrait in Photographs, The (Obolensky), 101

Sahadeva, 3, 4, 5
Salammbô (Flaubert), 52
Salzburg Festival, 116
Sanskrit, 25
Santanu, 2, 4, 5, 86
Sarabhai, Mallika, 75, 90–1, 104, 119, 120
Satie, Erik, 40
Satyabhama, 4
Satyavati, 2, 4, 5
Schlöndorff, Volker, 49
Scofield, Paul, 32, 40, 145, 150
Scotsman, The, 79
Seneca, Lucius, 39
Sentimental Journey, A (film), 30
Seweryn, Andrzej, 73, 80, 86–9
Shakespeare, William, 35, 36, 38, 40, 43, 45, 49, 69, 78, 79, 134, 141
Shakespeare Our Contemporary (Kott), 35
shakti, 91
Shakuni, 3, 6, 7, 22–3, 24
Shakuntala, 4
Shamba, 4
Shankar, Ravi, 110
Sharmishtha, 4
Shifting Point, The (Brook), 143, 147
Shiva, 7, 10, 56, 60
Shorter, Eric, 78–9
Shuru, 4
Sikhandin 9
Simon, John, 72
Singapore, 118
Singh, Shanta Serbjeet, 115
Smith, John D. 60–1
Soma, 4
Spain, 26, 112, 116
Sri Lanka, 109
Stahly-Vishwanadan, Antonin, 73, 98
Stanislavski, 42
Stayton, Richard, 69
Sterne, Laurence, 30
Stoppard, Tom, 49
Stratford Studio, 148
Strick, Joseph, 112
Subhadra, 3, 9
Subramaniam, 109, 110

Sun newspaper, 111
Sunday Times, 61, 79
Suprématie (Hugo), 51
Suzman, Janet, 148
Switzerland, 26, 112

Tabrizi-Zadeh, Mahmoud, 109, 110
Taking Off, 49
Tell Me Lies (U.S.), 38
Tempest, The (Shakespeare), 39, 40, 134, 148–9
Théâtre des Nations group, 39
Théâtre du Soleil, 69
Theatre of Cruelty, 36, 37, 148
Times, The, 78
Times Literary Supplement, 60
Timon of Athens (Shakespeare), 43, 47, 49–50, 53, 151
Tin Drum, The (Schlöndorff), 49
Titus Andronicus (Shakespeare), 33, 141
Tokyo, 79, 80, 112, 119, 120, 123
Torch Theatre, London, 30
Truffaut, François, 124
Tsuchitori, Toshi, 109, 110, 137
Tunis, 120, 121
Tunisia, 111
Turvasu, 4
Tynan, Kenneth, 32, 35, 145

Ubu (Jarry), 45, 109
Ulysses, 112
Unbearable Lightness of Being, The, 49
Union Bank of Switzerland, 118
United States of America, 26, 68
Universal Pictures, 112, 113
Upanishads, 51
U.S. (Tell Me Lies), 38, 69, 90, 145, 147
Uttara, 8

Vasudeva, 4
Vatsayana, Kapila, 118
Vayu, 3, 51, 52, 97
Vedic mythology, 51
Venice Preserved (Otway), 39
Victoria and Albert Museum, London, 104
Victorian Palace, Glasgow, 77
Vieux-Colombier, 41
Vigne, Daniel, 49
Virata, King, 8, 127, 134, 135
Vishnu, 3, 6, 60, 84
Vrishni, 4
Vyasa, 2, 4–7, 29, 59, 65, 74, 76, 97, 137, 143

Wagner, Richard, 79, 80
Wajda, Andrzej, 86
Wallace, Neil, 119
'War, The', 9–11, 26, 108, 127, 128, 136–9, *136*
Wardle, Irving, 38
Wars of the Roses (Shakespeare), 78–9
Weiss, Peter, 37
West End productions, 38
Westminster School, 30
Wilkinson, William, 73, 77, 111–12, 117, 118, 119, 144–5
Williams, Clifford, 148
Williams, David 50
Woolwich, Bishop of, 38

Yayati, 4
Yadu, 4
Yeats, W. B., 141
Yudhishthira, 3–11, 20, 21, 23, 61, 86, 88, 129, 131, 134, 141
Yugoslavia, 111
Yves Saint-Laurent International, 111

Zagreb, 120
Zeffirelli, Franco, 120
Zen Buddhism, 144, 147
Zürich, 55, 65, 66, 106, 111, 112, 117, 118